Storytools of Testing

The Most Unlikely Toolkit of a Testing Professional

Antti Niittyviita

Contents

Foreword

To find and unite a tribe of exceptional individuals who are willing to step up and take ownership of a cause. But which cause is it, you might ask?

In this case, the cause is the culture within software testing. You see, I believe that every team and every organisation needs their own champion of testing. Someone who will rise up to the challenge of leading the hearts and minds towards an exceptional testing culture.

I believe we meet here because we are destined to empower and inspire each other to share our best methods and tools for a common goal. Testing equals mental health because everybody's just happier when software works. This is why we need to pull our clients, colleagues and bosses out of the Matrix.

So are you ready? Join me on the quest and let's hack the testing culture together!

Introduction

It was way past midnight and the after party was going strong. We were just three boys sat around a table sipping their beers when the idea struck us. It was a larger than life idea, like most of the ideas that come after midnight.

> "Let's start a business. Become entrepreneurs and revolutionise testing."

Fortunately for us, we didn't foresee everything that was about to come. The financial crisis and everything that followed hit us hard. Maybe if we had, we wouldn't have started the business. Antti "Ato" Ojala, a good friend of mine, was already an academically exceptional guy with a masters degree in finance and engineering. He promised to set up the business, and we promised to follow him. In January 2006 he called and asked if I remembered the promise I had made? I didn't, of course, so he had to refresh my memory. A lot.

When I was little, my entrepreneur dad taught me that a man must always keep his word. It's like the old Navy SEAL proverb says, "We do not rise to the level of our expectation, we fall to the level of our training". I knew I had to keep my word to Ato. My father had trained me well.

So I quit my day job as a test and support manager and became the co-founder of Prove. A testing company made up of three friends in their twenties who were ready to reinvent their career paths from scratch again. It was a rocky ride for us. We were engineers who had no clue about sales, marketing, finance or running a business. Sitting in our 9 square meter office, we had to figure out what was the most valuable outcome of testing for the people we wanted to serve. Even more difficult was to figure out how to actually sell the idea to a stranger.

Our first business decision was to buy a cheap printer to print out our job contracts. We wanted the paperwork to feel official and it was a special feeling that day. In the first two years we managed to land 3 contracts employing a total of 9 friends. Then the day came. As the financial crisis took hold and all of our deals were cancelled within a month. We were screwed and we needed to regroup fast. I was a test manager back then, and all of a sudden I found myself in an emergency meeting. Ato had already been contemplating moving to another city with his family and had made his decision. He would stand down and pass the torch to whoever would step up. Nobody did, however and after a silence that felt like an eternity, all eyes turned to where I was sitting. "Could you do it? After all, your name is Antti too" they asked "Could you be the CEO?"

Little did I know that when I nervously accepted the torch, how tough it would be to lay off my friends, but it had to be done. That's how the new journey of discovery began for me. But what was I to do with a collapsed customer base and a dozen unemployed friends?

As the son of an entrepreneur, my first and only instinct was to meet with as many strangers in the software industry as possible and to ask what their most significant concerns were. Over the course of the next 10 years, I have met with more than 2200 people in the context of understanding their problems and finding out if they needed our testing services. It turned out that many decision-makers had mostly biased assumptions about testing rather than actual, hands-on experience. Their knowledge about testing was mostly taken from school books. They usually fell back on age-old habits of industrial management. They had no clue about the outcomes they wanted.

Most of the decisions were derived from the upper levels of organisation charts, which presented even more problems. I got faced with questions I had never thought of before. For example - What is the ROI of software testing? How can we make sure that our testing investments pay themselves back?

Being able to sell the simple idea of professional testing to a stranger presented a significant number of hurdles that had to be overcome. Making just one decision does not seem all that hard when perceived from the outside. But it is never a binary decision. It's never a decision if we should do testing or not. Basically, a stranger needs to decide not once but three times before anything concrete concerning testing will happen.

- Am I the kind of person who could invest time and money on testing?

- If I am, SHOULD I spend time and money on testing?

- If I should, what kind of testing should I choose to do?

It turns out that the tools we needed to close this gap, had very little to do with our skills as professional software testers. Too often, common sense was the least significant factor in decision making. It all boiled down to two fundamental features of the human mind. The beliefs people hold and the psychological defences they have. But how does one bypass those firewalls of the mind then?

Instead of studying yet another course or a book about software testing practices, I decided to set out on an expedition. For me, most of the essential tools we needed were hidden inside three books that don't mention testing at all.

- Influence by Robert Cialdini

- Start With Why by Simon Sinek

- How to Win Friends and Influence People by Dale Carnegie

But why would I consider these to be some of my most valued testing tools?

It's simple really. The results that we produce as testers only have value if others are willing to change their thinking, decision, or actions based on our work. For example by fixing a bug or re-considering release schedules. Regarding our business it all boiled down to helping others change their age-old mindsets about testing for the better.

Today, Prove is a company employing 46 testing gurus, and in our time we have sent out invoices totalling over €15 million for testing services. So it's safe to say that we have learned something along the way.

This book is a collection of tools that I have used the most in helping people change their mindset about testing.

Chapter 1

The Seeds of New Ideas

I love spicy foods. I especially love foods where I get to use the chillis that I grow myself. I plant the seeds of new varieties in February. The actual growth season is really short in Finland, so I've got to move early in the year if I want those juicy pods in August. The seeds, however, don't work their magic on their own. They need a lot of attention if they are to sprout, grow, flourish and eventually flower. Without attention, they wither and die. Naturally, with the right care in the form of water, light and nourishment the peppers grow into beautiful bushes that bear the fruit of my labour.

What I have learned over the years of growing peppers is that ideas work in precisely the same way. Ideas are the seeds of our circumstance, and they provide the crop, months or sometimes years later. But they only work their magic if we give them enough care and attention. Seeds are easy to transport. Sometimes I send chilli seeds to friends in an envelope. Sometimes I give away the seedlings in a small cup of soil. But how do I hand over the ideas that I consider worth planting in someone else's mind?

I deeply dislike the word but I have to say it here "communication." To me, the word "communication" is much like the word "strategy". It is void of any practical meaning for many of us. A word that puts a screensaver on people's faces in a conference room.

> "Now let's communicate our strategy process and business values."

Can you feel it? I immediately feel slightly nauseous and frustrated just writing those words for you. So let's substitute communication with something more fruitful.

The key to transferring and planting the seeds of new ideas is in speaking, writing and showing. It's in our being, from our thoughts to our words and to our deeds. However, the interface for all this is extremely delicate, and we need to discuss each component separately. Planting the seeds of ideas is an art like no other. It is an art that lies at the heart of all professional and personal success.

The Evolution of the Brain

All of the children stop playing, laughter, running and screaming as soon as the teacher stands up, clears her throat and utters a few simple words. We see the same phenomenon in a room full of grown-up conference guests when a skilled speaker adjusts the microphone and steps forward. So what is that magic spell that I talk about? What are the magic words that have such a profound effect?

The first human to walk the earth upright was Homo Erectus. The fossil skulls dating back 1.8 million years demonstrate that the early versions of the brain were on average only a bit larger than other species of ape. A little over 600ml to be more precise. By the time early Homo sapiens emerged, 300,000 years ago, the brain had doubled in size to 1200ml on average[1]. The curious thing is that the brain has not seen any significant growth in size after that. Although the complexity of tasks that the brain can handle has increased, there hasn't been any major developmental increments for the brain in over 50.000 years[2].

Although you might not the biggest fan of anthropology, the evolutionary history of the brain serves as the basis for everything that follows, so stay sharp now!

The Triune Brain Theory

I invite you to stay sharp now because one of the best-known models for understanding the brain is derived from its evolutionary history. The popular triune brain theory was developed by Dr Paul MacLean in the 1960s. According to Dr MacLean, the brain has a three-layer structure. To demonstrate the responsibilities of each layer, I ask you to picture this in your mind.

"It's a cold and dark night. The smell of approaching rain fills the air. Leaves have already turned yellow, and they cover the moist surface of the asphalt. The ground seems to swallow up the flickering light cast by the street lamp. The tension in the air manifested into pillars of steam as it meets exhalation. Just briefly, the cloud cover reveals the last glimpse of pale moonlight before the rain comes. The Predator waits. It knows that the younglings will be coming tonight. It has happened before, and it will always happen again and again. The Victim gives meaning to the existence of the Predator. Soon the taste of fresh blood would satiate the hunger. To kill is divine."

----

[1] Prof. John Hawks, Univ. Wisconsin

[2] Dr. Torkki & Power of Stories

The Reptilian Brain

The heart rate, breathing and body temperature are among the things that the brain controls on its own. It is automation of the highest order. You could willingly hold your breath until you pass out. But beyond that, the automation of life itself takes over, and breathing starts again. The oldest and deepest part of the human brain is what we call reptilian. It includes the same structures that are found in both reptiles and mammals. It is the part that helps us respond reflexively to our immediate sensory perceptions like falling or loud noises. If there are bodily sensations that emerge as a result of the predator story above, this is the part of the brain that responds to it.

The exciting thing from a human perspective is that the Reptilian brain responds to our memories and constructed mental images almost as

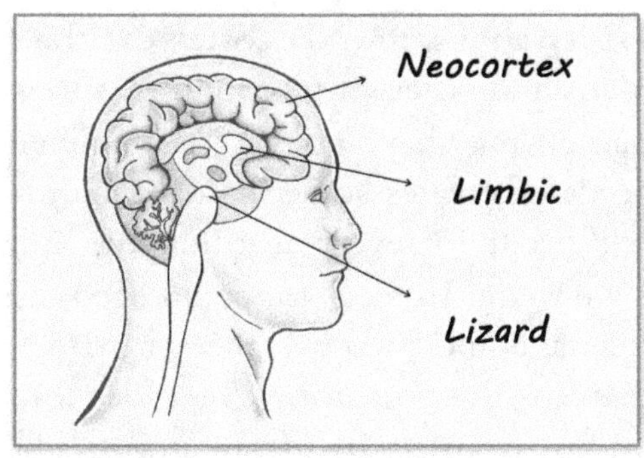

profoundly as it does to the real stimulus. Have you ever woken up in the middle of a dream all shaken up, sweaty and almost exhausted? The mind is inseparably connected to the body. You can try it out by thinking about how it would feel if you bit deep into a cold and juicy lemon. For most of us, such thought alone will trigger salivation.

The Limbic System

Inspiration, emotion, learning and memory originate in the mid layer of the brain. The Limbic system emerged in the first mammals, and the curious thing is that it has no capacity for language. The limbic system controls the motivations and value judgments we often make unconsciously. Therefore it exerts a strong influence on our behaviour.

Stories, like the one I told about the predator, resonate with the mental images both remembered and constructed. Pennywise, the Clown in Stephen King's IT, resonates through the limbic system deep into the reptilian brain too. That is why horror movies have the potential to generate physical reactions so easily. The same thing happens to us during moments of high social pressure such as public speaking for example. The limbic system has the power to trigger the fight or flight reactions, and it also plays a vital role in the genesis of phobias. The limbic system attaches the emotion to our experience, and the reptilian system conjures the physical reactions.

The Neocortex

Language, abstract thought, imagination, and consciousness mostly originate in the Neocortex, the youngest area of our brain. The neocortex is the part that we first see when studying an intact brain. It has two large cerebral hemispheres that play a dominant role. The neocortex is flexible and has almost infinite learning capabilities.

When I decided to write the Predator story above, my Neocortex did the job of arranging the words in a certain order, in an attempt to conjure up mental images that I could transfer to you. As you may have noticed, the deliberate vagueness in the way I described the predator creates some mental pictures in your mind. Those images tend to be different for everyone, and they might even differ for you if you read the passage again. In fact, you could even test it out by letting a few friends read the passage and then ask them to describe their mental image of the predator. What was the predator? What does it look like? Is it an animal or a human? Is it old or young? The mental images about the predator are that primal part of the brain at work. Words only point toward the meanings we already hold in our minds.

The reason I insist on explaining the triune brain is that it's seamlessly bound to all human interaction, influence and decision making. The idea that I want to share is something that crucially changed my perception about all communication inside software development teams. For me, the understanding was so profound that I genuinely wished I had come up with it myself. But the truth is, we tend to need teachers. Oren Klaff was the author and entrepreneur who finally opened my eyes to the idea. He wrote a fantastic book called "Pitch Anything" about his experiences closing hundred million deals with investors.

From my Inbox to Yours

As a software professional trying to communicate his way through teamwork, I was mostly like a bull in a china shop. My mistake was a simple assumption that eventually made a world of difference. When I make an Excel spreadsheet and send it to you, you will probably open that file with Excel at your end. Now the engineer in me always assumed that human interaction works in much the same way. And boy, did I make mistakes based on that idea!

In human interaction, the message that I want to deliver to you is formulated by my brain in the Neocortex. The Neocortex is the youngest area of our brain where language, abstract thought, imagination, and consciousness for the most part originate. I then transfer the newly-coded message to you by the medium of speech or maybe writing. My mistake had always been to assume that others will open and interpret that message with similar tools at their end, just like a spreadsheet.

It is true that the Neocortex might decode the words and the other communication cues we receive, but the actual meaning of the message emerges from somewhere else, buried deeper in the brain. A much older and deeper part of the brain stores all the meaning, emotion and memories those newly decoded words have for us. The limbic system is responsible for how you feel about what I say. That's why all the reason in the world might not convince us if the new idea just doesn't feel right.

The Opposing Forces of New Ideas

The brain, in its evolution, is hardcoded for survival and reproduction. Those areas of the brain have a keen ability to spot danger and predict threats, everywhere we go. They have deeply rooted beliefs, habits and defence mechanisms for protection. We might, for example, call them scepticism, boredom, doubt and sometimes even extreme things like a phobia.

It wasn't before I heard Sir Richard Branson tell his story on stage at a business conference, that I got the first glimpse of my personal defence mechanisms.

A hoard of disappointed travellers were sitting at the airport in Puerto Rico. Their flight had just been cancelled, and there were no alternatives available. When a young entrepreneur took up a blackboard and wrote:

> "$39 One way to BVI"

> "I had a beautiful lady waiting for me in The British Virgin Islands" said Sir Richard Branson as he discussed his motives for hiring a plane. That was the first flight of Virgin Airlines, but it wasn't to be the last.

To me, the story of how Virgin Atlantic came to be, is one of the most inspiring ones. I just love the rock'n'roll attitude Sir Richard demonstrated that day, but there is a more profound insight hidden as well. Over the decades the Virgin empire has grown into a 20 billion euro business across many sectors ranging from travel, entertainment, lifestyle to financial and healthcare to name just a few. The critical insight for me has been a quote that I initially heard Sir Richard say in a conference.

> "Doubt kills more dreams than failure" [3]

As a tester, I always valued the power of doubt and critical thinking. However, after getting to know the Virgin Empire and Sir Richard through a few of his keynotes and books, I had no other option than to revise my values. It turned out that doubt and scepticism were things that I personally used most often as excuses. It is emotionally easier to scrutinise the ideas of others than to present views of your own. It is far easier to watch the game on the bench and shout instructions to others than to actually play the game. It is far easier to be the critic than to say "Here. I made this. What do you think?"

---

[3] The quote is originally from Suzy Kassem, author of the book Rise Up and Salute the Sun.

When the conference crowd blocked the cloakroom entrance, I was left speechless in my seat. Sir Richard's words hung in the air as I wrote them on the cover of my diary.

> "Doubt is the enemy of new ideas."

But why is this story so important? Telling somebody, something, doesn't work. Considering such defence mechanisms as doubt, is it any wonder why "I told you so" is such a common notion in software projects that crash and burn? It's hard to change someone's thoughts or behaviour by merely telling them. Most likely the told-you-so will only serve to reinforce the mental defences. Telling is the equivalent of sending someone an Excel spreadsheet and assuming they interpret it alone with their Excel and nothing else. The app of language in the neocortex runs on the operating system of the limbic brain. In engineering terms, the API calls that go on between the systems inside a brain must not violate the OS level protections.

Let's do a little thought experiment. Imagine that you have never heard about Scrum before? Then someone came to you with a pitch.

> "Hey there! Use Scrum. It's a project management method that will make your development process 25% more efficient and impact positively on the stakeholder-satisfaction."

How did it make you feel? How did it sound to you? To me, there is a lukewarm feeling of "Meh. Can we get back to work asap?" Now let's consider a different kind of approach.

> "I love Rugby, and I think that we could learn something from it. Yes, I admit that the game is highly combative by nature, but maybe that is precisely why the team bonds are so strong in Rugby. One example of this is the New Zealand All Black Haka. It's a ritual performed at the beginning of

every game. What the team does is a traditional Maori war dance designed to bring the tribe together before the showdown. I believe that a real sense of team spirit and cooperation emerges when a team faces up to the trials of the game together. And these kind of habits and rituals are the key to sustained success. That is what I believe the Scrum method in software development is all about. Wanna hear more?"

Does it feel different? To me, there is a subtle sensation of curiosity and intrigue combined with an actionable mental image of athletes grouping together for a series of pre-game high fives and a serious discussion of the winning tactic.

The human version of effective communication should begin by talking to the limbic operating system first and disarm the danger seeking lizard brain. Only then, will the ideas that are the most significant, have a chance of passing through to the neocortex.

The Next stage of Evolution

The biological evolution of our genes got outpaced by a far more powerful force around 70,000 years ago. Yuval Noah Harari calls this milestone the cognitive revolution in his brilliant book "The Sapiens". Supposedly a genetic mutation altered the hardwiring of our species in a way that it enabled our ancestors to develop a new level of cognition. This sudden leap of evolution gave us a set of tools to both think and communicate things, real and imagined.

It's no wonder that so many religions describe the origin story of the world and mankind as the power of words. In fact, even the Bible describes in a very specific way.

> "In the beginning was the Word, and the Word was with God, and the Word was God."
>
> John 1:1

The power of words gave us an edge like no other. Biological evolution had to stand aside from a more powerful force that some call the cultural evolution. Humans are the only species on the planet that pass down both their genes and their understanding of the world. This understanding comes in the form of experiences, ideas, myths and beliefs. With this ability came rapidly growing cooperation which allowed the species to outpace Neanderthals, wipe out hostile animals and pave the way to developing agriculture as well. As it now seems, the evolution of culture has set us on the path towards the very stars.

Through the gift of the neocortex, children learned to listen to the teachings of the elders, they learned not to eat the poisonous mushrooms and were thus, more likely to survive. Those younglings didn't wander into the area where the lions lived, so they, in turn, survived to reproduce. The ability to listen and learn from the information of others was a crucial turning point in human evolution.

Now, let's consider a fireside chat among some imaginary cavemen. How does the timeless tribal wisdom get transferred to the younglings? The key to transferring the seeds of ideas are the simple words that can pause the running and laughter of kids. They are the words that will make a room full of conference guests lean in and fall silent. The tribe gathers around a campfire.

"Once upon a time..."

"It was a dark and stormy night…"

"I have a confession to make…"

"A week ago something curious happened to me..."

"Once, a friend of mine had an accident that nearly
killed her..."

It is no accident that the great sages of our times ranging from emperors to dictators, or from religious gurus to business leaders all tap into the same source. They use fables, parables, metaphors, analogies and epics to demonstrate the ideas they want to share. And sometimes out of those storytelling tools emerge the Twitter-friendly quotes we have all seen in motivational posters online. Human beings are highly sensitive to stories. Stories summon a field of mental images that engage the primitive parts of the brain first, the ones that are responsible for our unconscious judgements, intuition, motivation and emotions. These are the parts where our beliefs, values and mindsets also reside. It's as much a physiological mechanism as it is cognitive.

From a tester's point of view, is it any wonder that when it's time to make decisions, telling someone to test early and often seems to have no impact at all? It's the told-you-so-moment once more. Telling is an attempt to influence someone from the outside, and their defence mechanisms work quickly to swipe away new ideas. It's like trying to ping someone behind a firewall. First, you need to have an open port to do that. Stories are the Trojan Horse of communication because they have a tendency to do their work from within.

I once believed that storytelling was total nonsense in a professional environment. But after having gone through over 2200 meetings with strangers, I've had to revise that belief. Today, stories are the most essential tool that I use to make an impact and to help people change their testing practices. I met a CEO of one company five years ago and just last week I bumped into him again at a conference. He confessed that he doesn't remember my name, but he still recalls the story about blueberries that I told all those years ago. "It was a story about two buckets of test results" he admitted laughing "checking and hunting!" Engaging stories make the tools and ideas more accessible to recall, and they help others tap into the same resource as well. Stories make difficult concepts easy to transfer, and they are a stealthy way to plant the seeds of ideas into the new soil.

But what is it that makes a story good and gives us a chance to create a tool out of it?

What are the building blocks of Storytools?

Chapter 2

Start With Why

I have to admit. He has been my biggest man crush ever since the talk at the Nordic Business Forum, and it seemed like the rest of the audience agreed. All 7500 business leaders in attendance were completely silent when Simon started to speak.

> "I believe my purpose is to inspire people to do the things that inspire them so that, together, we can change our world."

I was blown away by the talk. For most of my life, I had been that left-brain guy who relied upon cold logic, reason and analytical thinking. An engineer to the core, some would say, with loads of Excel sheets thrown in for good measure. All of that was spiced up with a fistful of scepticism and cynicism. I must have been unbearable at times.

Six years before the talk, I had a life-changing meeting with Simon, although he probably doesn't remember it. The meeting took place on my laptop with a TED-talk video. By accident, I had found his amazing Ted talk entitled "How great leaders inspire action". That 15-minute talk changed the way I see the world, and it changed the way I think, communicate and act. The questions he posed have intrigued me ever since.

> "How do you explain when things don't go as we assume. Or better. How do you explain when others are able to achieve things that seem to defy all of the assumptions?"

Standing Out

It makes no difference if you love or hate Apple, it is indisputable that they are a stellar business. In fact, they are the most valuable company on Earth, beating Amazon by 149 billion dollars in 2018. Just as a side note here. The market value of Apple was 926 billion dollars in October 2018. With that amount of money, you could run the whole country of Finland for 14 years.

Everybody knows Apple, and most people have an opinion about them. The indifferent population is surprisingly thin, and to me, this notion holds exceptional merit just by itself. Apple is an easy example of the principle that Simon Sinek presents.

If Apple were a computer manufacturer like any of the others, they would say something like this.

> "We make great computers. They are beautifully designed and easy to use. Wanna buy one?"

It is something that Dell or HP might say as well. With it comes a sense of indifference. Why should I care about this specific idea or product? How Apple communicates instead, feels somehow different. You can try it for yourself:

"Everything we do, we believe in challenging the status quo. We believe in thinking differently. The way we challenge the status quo is by making our products beautifully designed, simple to use and user-friendly. We just happen to make great computers. Wanna buy one?"

The message in both examples is basically the same. Great computers that are both beautiful and easy to use. So what is it about the second approach that engages differently? The example either feels compelling or repulsive depending on what we think about Apple and their core idea of Thinking Differently. But there are subtle emotions connected to it, either way.

It turns out that those who really stand out at what they do, whether they are

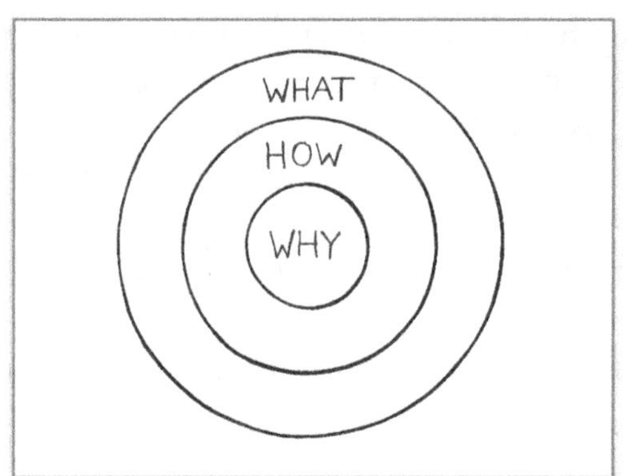

businesses or people, seem to have a curious way of structuring all of their communication. Simon describes it as the Golden Circle principle. The basic idea is almost embarrassingly simple, but at the same time, it is one of paramount importance. The Golden Circle principle is most naturally illustrated by painting a picture of a bullseye with three circles in it. Go ahead, you can imagine the bullseye here. The outer layer would be labelled with What, the mid-layer would be marked with How and at the core would be the Why.

Most of the people and businesses who have escaped the gravitational pull of the average, communicate in the exact reverse order from the rest of us. The majority of people start from the outer ring of the bullseye. They always know what they do and do a decent job in describing it too.

"I am a software tester"

"I'm a stay-at-home-dad"

"I'm an athlete"

"I study for a masters degree in economics"

Some people have the skill to go even deeper than the level of What. They can even explain the How of their What too.

"I mostly use Selenium and Postman"

"I exercise 5 times a week. Aerobic mostly"

But why should anybody care? Why are you are a tester? A stay-at-home-dad? Athlete? Student? What is it that drives you out of bed in the mornings? If you start with What & How, other people will have a hard time buying into what you do. It is a "rare export" to actually know and feel with certainty the driving forces behind our actions. That is the thing standing at the centre of Simon's circles, the WHY.

What is so different between the average and the stellar success stories then? According to Simon, those individuals and businesses always start their thinking, talking and doing in reverse order considering the bullseye. They begin with the WHY and only then move outward to the HOW and finally, the WHAT.

"People don't buy into what you do, they buy into why you do it."

Martin Luther King Jr. gave his world-famous talk on capitol hill on Aug 28. 1963. It was a talk that had been through hundreds of revisions and rehearsals across the American continent and at that specific moment in time over 250.000 people gathered to see Mr King give the talk. No Facebook event invitations, no Snapchat or Instagram to market the speech. Just word of mouth to rally the masses. But do you remember the name of the talk Martin Luther King Jr. gave that day? It wasn't the "I have a PLAN" speech that everybody remembers. It wasn't a talk revolving around the what and the how of civil rights. It was a talk about a dream that had been brewing for a long time, and Mr King gave a voice to the feelings of a nation. He gave a voice through a powerful speech that started with the Why.

Every successful idea or a speech like the one King gave on Capitol hill has a powerful "Why" behind it. But at the same time, they need a compelling structure. Something that might sustain the interest and attention of the audience in a world where attention spans grow shorter by the day.

First, let's consider this killer script. The most boring story imaginable

> "There once was a guy whose life was just great. He had an exciting job and great relationships in his life. After a while, his life got just a little better. He got a raise and got married. At the end of the story, everything was just excellent. His investments had paid off, and he had a chance to retire to his two passions, travelling and photography. What a perfect conclusion to a perfect story?"

Wouldn't you just die to see that kind of a movie? I wouldn't! I'd be bored out of my mind. A good story always has a beginning, a middle and an ending. It starts with a glimpse into the everyday life of a Bilbo Baggins or a young Skywalker. Then something unexpected happens, and the reluctant hero gets drawn in to the daring adventure that awaits.

Every engaging story has challenges and may even have antagonists too. After the heroic deeds are done, we are brought to the fulfilling conclusion. There is always a vision of a better tomorrow.

So how could we apply this idea in something practical like our professional summary in Linkedin or on the CV?

How to pitch your profession

Have you been to a dinner with friends or maybe a party when someone asks the traditional conversation starter

"So what do you do?"

The deep silence seemed to follow my response everywhere

"I'm a software tester."

For me, the question was mostly a conversation killer and not a starter. Why would anyone be interested? Especially outside of our domain, who cares if I was a coder, test automation specialist, or a support manager for our product line? There was no common ground for the conversation to continue. I had accepted the fact that software testing was one of the most unsexy businesses around, so I had reverted to vaguely explaining that I work with software.

But how could we find common ground even with very different professional backgrounds in this setting? Could there be points of interest that we still share here? We are good at parroting the title that is printed on our business card or the organisation chart. It is the What we do, and to me, it has become an easy way out. Sometimes people come up with quick answers just to make the question go away.

As the bestselling author, philosopher and a professional success coach Jim Rohn once said: "reasons come first, answers second." That is why I find it very interesting how common ground is just one word away from the original question. But before we go into that, let's dig a bit deeper.

The Magic Structure

By choosing the easy way out, we mostly dismiss the two essential components that constitute the majority of a successful pitch, presentation, talk or an idea. The structure is a tool for impromptu speaking situations as well, like a job interview or a toast at the party. And yes - for testing professionals, it might become a valuable pattern of reporting too.

What?

So what?

Now what?

I did not number the list for a reason, although it has been taught to writers and storytellers throughout ages. My purpose is simple. These questions have a specific order that has the most impactful in human communication.

WHAT? Is the introduction that establishes the context of our idea. It does not mean an information vomit of all that we know, but to give enough for the conversation to continue. The "what" might even be the everyday life of Bilbo Baggins or the young Skywalker in our story. An invitation to adventure. A call to action which the hero, of course, initially rejects. If you were a reporter composing a story for your magazine, you might ask things like:

What is the challenge we are facing here?

How did we get here?

What is the occasion we are celebrating here?

What is the position of the audience here?

What is it about this situation that is good/bad?

Now our hero is called forth onto the adventure. But why should the hero care? Why should anybody care? Our structure remains incomplete if we leave out the crucial part of "So what?"

SO WHAT? This is the part of our structure that to me seems most difficult. Let me give you an example. I've met with many testing professionals who wonder why it isn't enough that we just do an excellent job in finding bugs and reporting them on Jira?

I believe that the results of our work are only as good as the impact it makes on others. If nobody is willing to change their thinking, decisions or actions, based on the results we provide; is there any point in doing the work in the first place? So how could we help others to become more interested in our results?

> "Most of our results magically become interesting to others when we first become concerned with what interests them."

By understanding the motivations of others, we pave the way to serve our work and its results in an engaging way to others. The reporter within you might use questions like these to move forward:

What emotions are engaged here?

How does it make people feel?

What implication does our idea have on their life?

Which critical questions does this idea now pose?

Are there conclusions that we might draw here?

Now let's consider our hero again. There is an adventure ahead. The hero has taken heed of the calling or got forced into it. No matter which way it happened, there is a reason and motivation to follow through. So what should we do with the One Ring? What should we do about the Philosopher's Stone or the Holy Grail? Our structure remains incomplete if we leave out the last part of "Now what?"

NOW WHAT? This is the part we mostly forget. Considering testing reports for example. I only rarely see ones that remember to propose next steps that the testing team should take. Similarly, we might have a massive set of data generated by the load- and performance testing sessions but what should we do about the information? What are the conclusions and actions afterwards?

Our ideas consistently fall short of their full potential, and at the same time, we resign from our ownership if we don't learn to propose next steps. We must convert our conclusions and motivations into go-forward actions. And if we don't do it, one of two things will happen: Nothing OR Someone else will tell us what to do next. Either way, the seedling of our idea will wither and die.

If you were the reporter for the third time now, you might want to brainstorm questions like these to get started:

> Where could this reflection lead us in the future?

> How should we apply the ideas learned or discovered?

> What should we do differently the next time?

Finally, the hero sets out on the quest to save the world or the Prince held captive in the tower. The idea has been set in motion.

The Pitch About Testing

So let's get back to the pitch of our profession. At the dinner table or the parties, testing felt like the most unsexy profession imaginable. But the thing is that the question of "What do you do?" is an opening line voiced by the Neocortex. From your Excel to mine. And the basic instinct for an engineer is to match that. From my inbox to yours. The neocortex, however, is not the sexy part of the brain.

Shortly after seeing the talk that Simon gave, I visited the ICT Expo in Helsinki. It is an exhibition where business executives and ICT professionals meet and service providers exhibit their offering. The same question comes up hundreds of time in such a setting with slight variations like

"What does your company do?"

The small tester in me got curious at the event. Could we do some experimenting here with hundreds of candidates for a new kind of professional pitch? Indeed it was one of the most prolific experiments of my professional career. These days, wide but curious eyes stare back when the first sentence is left hanging in the air.

"Mental health. I do mental health."

"Mental health is our business"

The first responses of CIO's and CEO's at the ICTExpo were funny. "Huh?! So why is it that you are here at the exhibition then?" they asked.

"Well let me ask you. How does it make you feel when an app or a piece of software just doesn't work when you need it?

It is frustrating, isn't it? You see, my job is to help the developers by hunting the bugs before you need to suffer them. I do software testing. To me, testing equals mental health. Everybody's just happier when software works."

Laughter and personal stories about malfunctions of Outlook this morning were the most common feedback I got with this approach. My professional pitch had become a conversation starter instead of a killer. This time around, everybody had a new and very personal opportunity to relate to the grand story of software testing.

A successful and compelling story about your profession, or basically anything you'd like to pitch, has three critical ingredients as Simon Sinek put in his brilliant book "Start With Why." And this book is the reason I decided to hack the order of our magic structure of What? So What? Now What? This is it.

The WHY:

Remember how I said earlier that the common ground is just one word away? This is it. People don't buy into what you do, they buy into why you do it. This is "A beginning" that captures the interest of your audience. It establishes a shared point of view for both of you to explore further. That is what mental health stands for in my example.

The HOW:

This is how I execute on the reasons we share. Here I describe the way I approach the idea or the problem. In this example, the tester is the bug hunter who catches the bugs before you as a user need to suffer them. A tester helps software developers to succeed ever better.

The WHAT:

Finally comes the wrap-up aimed at the Neocortex. The ending tells what I do. Simply put, software testing is my profession.

Now, if you've ever seen great stand-up comedy shows, there is an exciting feature within the best jokes. They frequently revisit previous stories, feeding on their funniest parts. The narration of outstanding comedy tends to make loopbacks. This is a way to make any pitch intellectually more intriguing.

In the pitch about our profession, I might want to loop back by explaining how happiness equals mental health to me. Everybody just feels better when software works, no way to argue with that. With the Start with Why approach, we can immediately step up a level in our influence. No matter what the content is that we deliver, the impact it has on others is at the basis of all value.

> "Your content grows in value fast, by creating some emotionally engaging context first."

The same principle applies everywhere we communicate. Be it a regular testing report or a pitch of our profession in an interview. The same structure could even be used to each entry of your career path on the CV.

The Pitfall of Why

There is one risk to using "Why", however. Imagine a situation when you were a teenager. You had promised to come home no later than 10pm on Friday. You know that you are hours past the deadline when returning home that night. Trying to sneak in through the door is useless because dad is sitting there at the kitchen table waiting for you. You didn't even pick up his calls this time.

> "Why are you late?!"

He asks with a deep voice. And you know that there is trouble ahead.

"Why" is a question which tends to kick off a series of explanations instead of the real reasons. In a much different setting it evokes excuses like - there was just too little time to get started, the tools did not work, the process is our problem, the organisation does not support us, the political state of the world is so unstable and besides it was raining like hell too and the traffic was terrible. The excuses always seem to fall outside of our control. For this reason "Why" is a dangerous question to ask, and a difficult one to answer.

Sometimes the seeds of ideas can take a decade to sprout and ripen into a bountiful crop. For me, it took six years. Simon Sinek's talk at the Nordic Business Forum in Helsinki finally connected the dots for me in a simple realisation. What if, instead of asking why, dad could choose another way? You enter the door at midnight again. But this time he smiles gently.

> "Hey there. I was worried. What was it about tonight that was so important to you, that you were willing to sacrifice our cooperation this way?"

The tone changes immediately. In skilled hands the "What" becomes a question that eventually guides us to the true source of the "Why".

The structures described in this chapter can be deployed in any scale and shape to most of our thinking, communication and even action. Making use of these ideas means implementing an entirely new skillset on top of our traditional technical testing skills. It's not going to be easy, but I believe the rewards far exceeds the sweat of pushing through. This is a process that we could start right now with this book if you decide to find out how deep the rabbit hole is. So are you with me? Shall we commit to it all the way to the end? Not just by knowing, but by doing too?

Alright. You're still reading. I assume you've made a decision! Respect! Now, let's move on.

Applying the Structure

Just recently Jeff Weiner, the CEO of LinkedIn said something about the job market in his home country. He said that the most significant skill gap in tech currently is in the soft skills. And I have to agree with this. Our ability to influence people, defines how the results of our work will impact others. The effects of our work is the main thing that matters. The results of our work either wither and die or spark into magnificent life by the skill we have in communication. Because of this, I've even begun to contemplate a concept I like to call feedback-driven testing.

But testing is always a feedback-driven process, right? Of course, we see testing as a constant dance of inputs and feedback.

It's only natural since most of us are Neocortex oriented. The behaviour of the product at hand is our feedback for the inputs we make. Due to our techy orientation to work, we have become really good at bug centric reporting too. It's only natural because bugs are a big deal in our thought, our word and our work. At the same time, we easily overlook the fact that bugs are the WHAT of our communication. The problem in bug-centricity is that we quickly forget the WHY and the HOW of our communication. Those two components which have the most significant contribution to the impact we make on others, as we mentioned earlier. Our results are useless if nobody is willing to change their thinking, decisions or actions based on them. Instead of results-thinking, we would need impact-thinking.

On a regular basis, I meet testers frustrated at their clients, colleagues and bosses. They keep asking questions like:

> "Why is it that nobody cares about the results we produce?"

> "Why is it that all the bugs we find are deemed trivial or features instead of things to be fixed?"

We might even think we deliver outstanding outputs from our testing, but what if they make no one else tick the way they should? I believe that most of the time our clients, colleagues and bosses are not stupid, and they don't deliberately ignore the efforts of testers. I think that there are only two possible reasons why testers end up asking questions like these and both reasons are mostly in our hands.

The results of our work actually suck and we are doing the wrong things with our work time. Or the results of our work are actually useful, but we haven't found a way to make it engaging in an actionable way. Either way, it is our responsibility to fix issue. This is the approach I like to call "feedback driven testing". Feedback driven testing does not mean a feedback we observe in our software product, but feedback from the people we get to serve. My results will not be interesting to anyone unless I first pay attention to what interests them. That's the feedback I mean.

"Paying Attention Will Pay Off."

Observe the people around you and be curious about their motives, needs and desires. Your work is only as good as the impact it has on your customers, colleagues and bosses.

So let's recap quickly. We now know that we will need great results that we can deliver to the people we serve. Obvious, I know. But that's not all, in addition to that, we will need to continually pay attention to the people around us to understand what they are interested in and what lights them up. Once we understand that, we need to craft our interactions by starting with 'why', explaining the 'how' and only then addressing 'what'. With all that taken care of, the professional always concludes with a forward motion by presenting a 'now what'. This is the way to create an impact that in the end create the value for your results.

Now, I bet you're not surprised if I said that it's still not yet enough to go the whole nine yards.

There is a paradox at play.

The Ship of Theseus

There is a ship in port and it belongs to Theseus. It's just about to leave Athens for a really long sea journey. In fact, the journey is so long that spare parts need to be loaded in the cargo hold. Otherwise, we would be left with nothing but a wreck.

The ship needs repairing during the voyage and piece by piece, plank by plank it is renewed. Old parts are tossed over the railing as the new parts replace them. By the time it returns to Athens, every single piece of the ship has been changed. Now we are faced with the inevitable question of identity.

Is this new ship the same one that left the harbour so long time ago? And if not, when exactly did the ship change? This is actually a question that has been around for thousands of years. It's actually been a matter of thought for ancient philosophers like Heraclitus and Plato. Most people I know consider it to be the same ship. So now the dilemma grows more complex.

What if a bunch of pirates followed the original ship on its voyages and gathered every single piece of wood tossed overboard? What if at the time of return, the pirates then assembled the original ship. Now with two similar ships at the harbour, which one would be the real ship of Theseus? Difficult isn't it. There is a simpler variation the story too. It's about Lincoln's axe (or if you are a fan of British comedy, Trigger's Broom). This legendary axe is held in a museum, and over centuries it's head and shaft corrode. Eventually, the shaft has been changed to a new one several times, and the rusted axe head is switched for a new one too. So is it the same axe anymore? And what if some scavenger took the old parts from the trash and reassembled the original axe later?

Usually, at this point the answers start to diverge. It is not that simple anymore. In philosophy, it is called an identity paradox. In both scenarios, a new Ship of Theseus arrives in Athens, but only in the first scenario, it might still be considered the real one. The defining factor with the identity of this ship is the story it holds. It's a story we hold in our minds.

Have you ever heard the old saying that content is king? It is widely used in the world of business development and marketing. The saying refers to an idea where the content is the defining factor of value. In testing, for example, the content tends to refer to things like the documentation we produce or the bug reports we deliver. Now, this is where I've got to disagree. Content might be the necessary basis for all the value, it's true that without a ship to begin with, there would not be a paradox either. But content most certainly is not the king. The context that we create in the form of a story defines the way we see the actual outcome of this sea voyage. Similarly, the context defines the way we see the axe which once belonged to Lincoln.

The same principle applies to all of our work as professionals. Every single piece of content that we create is subject to the story people construct in their minds. This is why I say that the context is truly the king. But the story does not end there. Before the context, comes a void that lives in the core of our concepts.

The Core of our Concepts

I believe that words have the potential to pierce through the conscious mind. Let's think about something really simple first. For example the word "game". It is a homonym because it has multiple meanings. It would mean a different thing if you were in the forest on a hunting trip than if you were a gamer at a LAN party. A single word can conjure a world of mental images inside the minds of others. The language we use is vague by its very nature. It's like a game of "hide and seek". Let's try another word. Can you explain what a "room" is? How would you explain it to someone who does not know what a room means?

> "Well, a room usually has furniture, carpets, and decorations" someone might say. But is it so simple? Those are things inside the room, but they are not the room.

> "Well, a room has walls, a floor, and a ceiling" someone else might say. But is it so simple? Those things only draw the boundaries of the room, but they are not the room.

So, what is a room then?

The room is only space. We could even say that what is not there, the emptiness, is more important than what is there. And it's the same thing with even more abstract concepts like strategy or vision. We can always describe things that are included and the things that define the boundaries. But can we ever express what's in the heart of that concept other than emptiness?

I admit that we got on the philosophical side of the discussion there. And at the same time, it seems to me that this is what we forget in our strategy meetings, process workshops, and scrum retros most of the time. There is nothing at the core of our concepts. Yet, we talk about them with an assumption that everybody shares the same mind-scape.

Every word is a void which is filled up by the imagination of the person who hears it. Basically, it means that everything we try to describe through language is a crude simplification of reality, just as a spec is a speculation about what the real thing should do. Whether we are talking about writing, speaking or thinking, our language describes an unlimited amount of possibilities. And from that infinity it is the listener who finally decides the meaning for the words that you speak, it is the reader who ultimately decides the meaning for the words that you write. It's the receiving end of our communication who owns the show, so what could we do about it?

Clickbait and Testing Results

In my opinion, "I've given it some thought." is a pointless expression. Every day I find myself more confident that thinking for human beings is as automatic a function as blood circulation, respiration or digestion. The flow of thoughts is an uninterrupted film reel. It is an everlasting dialogue of either past or future. And, the majority of the mind's movie has nothing to do with what is actually at hand. Remember when we discussed how many thoughts go through an average brain in a day? The count varies between 35,000 and 75,000 depending on the research we find. And yes, I do have a friend who is convinced that her thought count is over 100,000 per day!

While working with limited knowledge, the mind has a habit of building framework information to support the content. A mathematician would call it interpolation, I call it storytelling. And, we are excellent at it. You can personally stop and give it a try. What kind of mental images does a clickbait story like this conjure?

Weekend: Triple homicide in Glasgow.

Snow inferno about to devastate Paris.

Financial Mayhem: Terror on Wall Street.

It can make our inner storyteller go wild. Take the first one for example. "Oh dear. What could have happened there? A love triangle maybe? Some booze or even drugs involved?" Even though getting wild is fascinating, it can also quickly become dangerous. Truth and circumstance are often forgotten. How would your mental images change if we were to consider an armed burglar and legitimate self-protection?

There is another thought experiment I love. Imagine it's late, and you're alone in the house. In the darkness, you work on the computer. Suddenly, slow footsteps at the door catch your attention.

How would that feel? What would you think?

That piece of information is the content, just like the ship of Theseus or Lincoln's axe. What do the footsteps mean? For most of us, the brain starts to work on the context of those steps immediately. Who could it be? Am I expecting someone? Does it feel creepy? Who has the key? Should I be alone or is there someone with me? Just a brief glimpse of information(content) kicks the brain into constructing a story(context) around it.

If I were a novelist capturing your imagination, that mechanism would be extremely beneficial for me. But how is it for a professional in other fields of expertise? Should a doctor let the imagination of the patient run free? Should a CEO let the imagination of employees run free? Should a software tester let the imagination of the product owner run free?

As a professional, I've consistently discovered that content without context is either useless or dangerous because it sets the imagination in motion. The same thing applies to most of our professional concepts too. Concept without a frame is either useless or dangerous. In my work, I don't want to let my bosses or client's imagination run free about what I've been up to this week at work.

So let's get back on the testing track then. As testers, we often make the mistake of only reporting on the bugs we find. That's the content part of the story. That's the Ship of Theseus and the clickbait headline. But where is the context of it all? While imagination is a great tool, I'd like to avoid it in a professional setting related to the results I provide.

Someone will always create the context for the content you've got. Luckily, you get to choose who is in charge. It could be you, or the mind of your audience. I'm actually willing to say that for professionals, the ownership of the interpretation is a prerequisite for success. Wow. Now that was a sentence with lots of long ambiguous words! I tried to say that there are two things a professional should consistently do to succeed.

Inhale: Master your own interpretations by gathering enough information about the context.

Exhale: Master your own communication by sharing enough information about the context.

Accepting your responsibility at both ends of communication will change the game.

Inhale: It's simple really. In testing, it is our responsibility to gather all the relevant information so we can later play our game of bug hunting to its full potential. How can we produce world-class results if we don't know enough about the context? So we need to use our curiosity by asking questions and our attention when downloading the information that we receive. That is how we master our interpretations.

Exhale: Let's think about another example. This is an easy way to experiment with your skills in the game of content and context. What would you be able to say about your testing if no bugs were found today? Stop now. Really think about it for 60 seconds! What would your report say if you were not allowed to talk about bugs at all?

Can you explain consistently why you did the testing in the first place? Can you tell how you did the testing? How did you come up with the results you have? By taking these kind of questions into account, you will be able to create the context for your content. To lead the imagination and the attention of those around you.

In a testing report, be it written or spoken, the story could begin by letting others in on the activities you engaged in during this testing session. You might want to tell them for example about the time allocated to activities like configuration, meetings, investigations, bug reporting and coverage. But can you elaborate even further by showing on a map which areas were covered and which were left out this time? It's clear once we stop and think about it. But hard when someone calls you and asks for a report while you're still engaged in the daily flow of action points.

That's why I invite you now to outline a new storyline for the moment the limelight hits you the next time. A pen, some paper and a short bullet journal might be all you need to make a difference. How would you construct the next report you get to deliver?

Questions & Actions: #1

How would you start your professional summary in your resume or LinkedIn profile if it had to start with words "I believe…."? I invite you to stop here and take a piece of paper. Use 5 minutes to brainstorm 10 crazy ideas that would fill up this sentence.

Questions & Actions: #2

Have you ever considered your bug or testing reports through the glasses of a creative writer? What if you tried out a storyline next time including answers to the following questions: Why did you do this session? How did you get the results? What did you find? Now what?

Let's recap the example pitch: I do mental health. You know how it feels when an app or a piece of software just doesn't work? At least it pisses me off, so I do my part by hunting the bugs before you need to suffer them. I do software testing and to me testing equals mental health. Everybody's just happier when software works.

Questions & Actions: #3

What information about context could you gather for testing assignments? Make a list of things to ask. Consider stakeholders, business, documents, testability, consider time and resources. What could you gather on these?

Questions & Actions: #4

Sharing your report, what could you tell about the content? What would you say if no bugs were found? How did you test? How did it go? What did you do? What didn't you do? How good was the testing? How is it connected to others? What next?

Chapter 3

How Does a Mindset Change?

First, let me give you the background. Let me place the point into context. We had a problem. A client of ours dismissed most of the bugs we delivered as minor or trivial things. We knew for sure that these bugs critically threatened the value of their product because most of what we found were minor or trivial things during the first five minutes of the boarding process to the new software. The setup wizard sucked big time. A new user faced with countless small but annoying bugs does not get a good first impression. In a customer market that is for sure, not a thing to wish for. The modern state of the internet exposes the truth, fast. No amount of marketing or advertising money can cover up the pain of a bad product. Seek online reviews for any product and you will understand what I mean.

We knew we had to do something to save our clients business since the product was about to hit the mass market in a few months on over a million devices globally.[4]

We booked a meeting with the board of directors in the project and started preparing. We needed a pitch that would open the eyes of our audience. Jerry, one of our executives back and gave us a perfect story to make our point. It was an everyday incident from the previous week..

It was an exceptional Monday in our office[5]. No one was on a business trip, and we all had time for a morning coffee together. "It's a great day today! My to-do list will be empty by lunch! Hahaaa!" said Jerry. Suddenly his phone rang. "Greetings from market research…'"said the voice. Then came a second call. "Top of the morning from the supporters of This-and-That. May I have a moment of your time?" said the guy. The coffee had time to grow cold, and then we got the daily mailbag. No, I don't mean email or the newspaper, we still get regular mail at times!

There had been some kind of logistics error at the post office, and one of the envelopes was just a ripped up mess of confetti. Contract papers from a customer were missing. It was time to pick up the phone again and investigate.

"It's lunchtime guys!" someone shouted at the front door.

"What?! Noooo!" shouted Jerry

"I haven't done a single item on my to-do list yet."

---

[4] The context illuminates our motivations and the situation that we are facing. In addition to that, it primes the mind to better understand the solution we came up with.

[5] Second, comes the content to which we just drew the frame. The following is the exact story that we practised and demonstrated to the board of directors of our client.

It was a typical morning when an abundance of annoying small things became the big thing. After witnessing what a frustrating morning Jerry had that day, I've never heard the famous sentence the same way again.[6]

"We don't need to fix this. It's just a small bug."

After telling this story, we prepared a fishbone diagram of the first five minutes of usage of the client's new device. In the picture, we had screenshots of all the views that the setup wizard would show to the end user and, attached to each of them we had every minor bug with a bright red colour. We printed out the whole diagram on a huge piece of paper and rolled it up like an ancient Egyptian parchment. When we unrolled the paper in front of the board, the expressions were priceless. Instantly we knew that we had nailed the presentation and made our point. Jerry´s story was a crucial part of the whole exercise. This is because a story does not attempt to inform people in the same way that a powerpoint presentation does. Instead, it primes the mind for the core idea to come. A story starts to live inside people and grows into an insight of their own. We only helped the insights to emerge with the board by sharing the story Jerry had and then made the idea concrete by demonstrating its relationship to their product that was about to meet millions of customers.

'We don't need to fix this. It's a small bug' was a sentence which soon became a joke in that office, and I hear they even printed a poster of it later to decorate the office wall. That's the power of insight. That's the power of a story.

The next time you come face to face with a mindset mistake like this, take a step back. Tell this story or one of your own. Be a tester and see what happens. Don't let a flock of small things become your big thing. Stories like this are a tool to start a discussion about those difficult topics. They are a tool to spark a change of mindset because most people have similar experiences with annoying mornings anyway. Especially Monday mornings!

---

[6] Third, comes the core points, meaning the conclusions and insights that we can draw from the content.

Now it's time to zoom out a bit. We've reached a turning point in the book. We meet here on this page regardless of the shackles of time and place. It feels fantastic to make this journey together. So, are you ready to proceed? The next part is going to be huge, I promise!

In the next chapters, I've collected a set of most typical mindset mistakes from my expeditions in the software industry. Based on the evidence of meeting and training thousands of people in testing and selling professional bug hunting services for over €15,000,000, I now know that these ideas work for us. The next step could be to figure out if they work for you too.

Most of the following mindset mistakes are especially common in executive level people who don't understand the core concepts of testing yet. At the same time, I've also met testers who have a hard time explaining to others what they do.

In order to wake up as many people as possible; to rethink their testing, I invite you on a journey through 11 mindset mistakes about testing.

Questions and actions #1:

Identify three situations or mindset mistakes your colleagues, clients or bosses have about testing. Things like "minor bugs don't need fixing". What are the typical conflicts with developers? How about managers? Does someone think that testing is a monkey job?

Questions and actions #2:

Think about three small and personal stories just like the one that Jerry gave us. Write the titles and a few significant details down. Then find a friend to practice with. Share one of your stories with them just for the fun of it. And tell them why you do it too.

Chapter 4

Mindset Mistake #1:

Testing Equals Quality Assurance

I was so excited. Two years into the project I was hired as the test manager for a project developing a state of the art touch screen smartphone that would revolutionise the world. "This is an opportunity of a lifetime!" I thought, when I got to meet the rest of the testing team on both continents. My client wasn't Apple so you might already guess that this is not going to be a success story, even though I thought so at the time. It was within our testing team that we got the first glimpses of the disaster that was to come.

I spent the first six months as the leading figure of the testing team. During that time, we witnessed two things happening simultaneously. On one side, our testing metrics were increasing rapidly. Our acceptance tests championed a pass rate of 98% and the feature owners cheered. At the same time, the mood of the testing team deteriorated, and the reason for that was apparent too. The real impression of quality that we experienced in our testing sessions was crumbling by the week.

When our testing team started to realise that we would never be able to make it, we repeatedly began to show the reasons to our board of directors. The owner of the product did come to the same conclusion, but it happened eight months later after we had wasted millions and millions of funding. I think that the decisive moment was when the CTO of the company got the latest prototype in his hands to get the look and feel of this amazing new smartphone. The screen even had haptic feedback so that tapping the screen would feel like pressing a button. Now that I think about it, it really strikes me as amusing that we moved away from real buttons and then wanted to make the screen feel like real buttons again! Well, back to the point! The only problem was that swiping the screen caused the haptic feedback to loop and the phone instantly became a vibrator when dragging a finger across the screen. With a little dildo in his hand the CTO looked stunned and forced a polite smile.

It was only the tip of our iceberg, obviously an inconvenient bug, but everything kind of worked according to our vague specification. So the product owner of the touchscreen and haptic feedback decided to call it a feature. That's how our test case pass rate was well over the 98% that had been demanded - and everybody got their annual bonuses.

The months that followed this incident were some of the most insightful of my career. We mercilessly went through issues and tried to find solutions in grand weekend camps of testing and fixing. And when we did not work, we attempted to squeeze in just enough sleep to get through the next day.

Finally, we started hearing the all too familiar questioning that testing professionals seem to face when trouble arises.

"Your mission is to assure the quality. You are quality assurance! Why does everything in this project go off the road? Don't you do your job?!"

I have to admit that Quality Assurance did sound grand. It looked great on our business cards as well! Too bad that it had little to do with testing. During the last months of the project, I learned more debating skills than ever before. I learned to deal with the mindset mistakes and assumptions that people who didn't know about testing were making.

The first mistake was one that even I had always made. I had thought that testing equalled quality assurance. During one sweaty night, I woke up again to the question.

"You are the QA! Don't you do your job?!"

It was just like in the movies. I sat up straight in bed - all sweaty. I occasionally entertain the idea that I probably was shouting as well, but that could be just my vivid imagination! The answers were laid out in front of me as I jumped out of bed to my journal where I started writing as fast as I could.

- Do testers control the source code?

- Do testers control development practices?

- Do testers control the project budget?

- Do testers control project schedule?

- Do testers control the shipment decision?

Mostly the answers are no, so why on earth would we want to call it quality assurance, when the ones doing it have no control over the quality?

This idea probably seems obvious to anybody involved with testing, but at the same time, it was powerful enough to drive me deep into the mindset mistakes people have about testing. Most mindset mistakes are evident to testing professionals and at the same time unseen by others. Quality assurance is a grand word, but it sets the mind on the wrong track right from the start. It implies control over the quality and those who have it on their business cards surely are the ones. Right?

Is it My Job or Ours?

We used to travel to Lapland every year with friends and family. Sometimes we had as many as 20 people in the group, so a small cottage wasn't enough. Nights were dark enough for us kids to play hide and seek with flashlights and the sauna was always ready when we finally decided to go inside. We looked forward to those trips for weeks!

We didn't like Sunday mornings at all, however. Before heading back home, we had to clean up the place. My task was always to clean the bedrooms with my friend. There was still lots of stuff to take care of, candy wrappers, potato chips, dust, and sand. Boooooring!

Once, we came up with an idea for a shortcut. We merely swept all the trash out of the bedrooms to the corridor, packed up our things and were ready to leave faster than ever. So to did all our friends on the other side of the hallway. Eventually, my dad opened the door to the hall to check if we were ready. A gust of wind rushed through the house and promptly blew the piles of trash back into the rooms, and we were back to square one! We didn't need another lesson on the second run. We bagged up all the trash at once to prevent the wind from making us do the job a third time.

I've seen this happen in software projects time and again. Teams tend to play the game to their ends, trying to make sure their bedroom is in order, and at the same time giving no thought to the corridor. Sometimes it is a matter of incentives. And other times it is about the organisational silos where we lose sight of the common goals along the way.

Basically, this is what happened to my fantastic touchscreen smartphone project as well. All of our feature teams, like the one doing the haptic feedback, were playing the game to their ends. It seemed that everyone did their part. But eventually, someone opened the door, and the gust of wind did the rest. It is never enough to just stick to our own stuff. Mostly we need someone to open the door early and wide enough to see if the big picture stands up to even the strongest of winds. And this to me, is where testing steps in.

Quality is a Team Effort

Let's consider a different point of view. Team sports for example. Scoring goals only wins the game if the defence supports the offence in a meaningful way and doesn't let in more goals than we score.

"When the team scores, everybody celebrates."

This holds true for software development too. A developer plays to score the big goals. The tester aims to support him by keeping the defence solid. Neither can succeed without the other. When the division of work is flawless, everybody appreciates it, including the adoring fans. No team in the world can outsource success to a single group of experts. A team solely playing offence is sure to lose.

"Quality is the responsibility of everyone."

The goal of testing is not to build confidence or to assure others. Testing is to produce information that supports both development and decision-making. And by doing just that, the actual mission of testing is to destroy all of the false confidence, in return for an opportunity for better products to arise.

> Testing tells the truth and nothing but the truth.
> Quality is something that emerges in its wake.

After realising that even though our job title was QA, we were not solely responsible for the quality. I started to breathe again. I felt like a weight had been lifted from my shoulders. But of course, the idea in my mind was only halfway there. I needed to learn how to explain it to others too.

Do you remember the old philosophical thought experiment?

> 'If a tree falls down in the forest, and no one is around to hear it, does it make a sound?'

The first impulse would be to say that it does. But let's dig a little deeper into the mystery. As the tree falls, air molecules begin to vibrate, and waves are created. As the wave propagates out from the tree at 343m/s, it either comes into contact with a person's eardrum - or it does not. If it does, then the person's eardrums vibrate, and a series of nerve signals get sent to the brain. The brain on its behalf takes time to categorise the message by comparing the perception with all its previous experiences. Memories in other words. Finally, our brain attaches a meaning to this series of events, and that is what we call a sound.

If there is no one there, the wave will continue to propagate outwards, and it eventually becomes absorbed by the forest. So in a way, the wave that is created by the falling tree only contains part of the story of the tree. For the story to be heard, there must be a person nearby who can receive the wave and convert its vibrations into the meaning we call sound.

This is true of our job as testers too. We can have the most detailed ideas, results and reports, but if we can't find a way to get them appropriately received, then they will suffer the same fate as the falling tree in an empty forest. They will never be truly heard. So we will need a set of tools to make those ideas stick. Quality is the responsibility of everybody, but I'm responsible for providing actionable information to my team and making sure it is heard! So that is why the stories, metaphors and analogies emerged, a few of which you have already been reading.

Testing is the Opposite of Something. But What?

Have you ever thought what the opposite of "belief" might be? It's not disbelief even though it might be the first impulse to say so. To believe is to place our trust in something that we are not sure about. It is a decision. For some of us, that belief might even be a decision about the ultimate anatomy of the universe.

On the other hand. If there were something that we could be entirely sure about, then there would be nothing for us to believe in. There would only be the opposite, which I like to call certainty. So I propose that certainty is the opposite of belief, and this is the truth. I give you my assurance! And notice how I do it with an exclamation mark too!

Doesn't it feel off when I try to assure you that this is the truth? Would you not like to question my logic further? Would you not challenge it if you were given a chance?

As we discussed earlier, testing professionals often seem to be in love with a notion of quality assurance. Even though the very word assurance generates feelings of unease and it makes us want to question it further. A rational human would want to test the logic behind those assurances. The verb 'To Assure' aims at creating a sense of certainty or confidence, but at the same time, it mostly succeeds in building beliefs that support our assumptions.

Instead of evidence to back up our assumptions, software development really needs observations that demonstrate the truth. That is why we actually need testing instead of assurance. Now that was a complicated way to explain a simple thing. Shame on me. Let me share a more straightforward way now.

Superheroes and Software Testing.

Do you remember Mel Gibson's Lethal Weapon movies? Or the ones where Bruce Willis just won't die? What about Tim Burton's gloomy and rainy Gotham City with the Bat signal shining hope under the hanging veil of clouds? Who ya' gonna call?

Action movies have throughout time had a plot that fascinates the imagination. Small time criminals creep around in dark alleys in the middle of the night from New York to Metropolis. Luckily for us, the police know their stuff. They enforce the law and make sure that day to day life is smooth. The job of Commissioner Gordon and his colleagues is to observe and patrol. To keep an eye on anything suspicious. Is the letter of the law followed? Are agreements respected? Everything goes smoothly until…suddenly, the peace gets shattered! It always does.

Enter a criminal boss, an arch nemesis, who displays his or her twisted, sneering, countenance. The criminals get organised for a fight, and the police are powerless to stop them. The fate of the city is hanging by a thread. Victory will not come cheap. One needs to take up dirty measures, and the hero needs to put her reputation on the line. Working in the shadows to catch the criminals might even make the police turn on the hero instead. Remember The Dark Knight? Vermin do not respect law or rules, so why should you as a tester?

The question boils down to two very different activities that hide under the umbrella-concept of testing, or sometimes quality assurance. But before revealing the mystery of those activities I've got a quote to make. I just can't help, but say it out loud here.

I just recently read an outstanding testing book that doesn't mention testing once. The book was called the 7 Habits of Highly Effective People written by the late guru Stephen R. Covey. Sold by the millions, the book is an invaluable tool for any professional planning for a level up. But the idea wasn't to advertise the book. I wanted to quote one of the seven habits here before proceeding. It was called Begin with the End in Mind. At first, it seems obvious, but in testing terms, there is profound wisdom to it.

Testing or Quality Assurance are both umbrella-concepts that hide two primary activities beneath them, and those activities produce very different results. When beginning with the end in mind, we must ask the difficult question first. What is the outcome that we expect from testing this week, today or this session? Why are we doing this? Too frequently I see projects that focus on doing testing right instead of testing the right things. It is easy to focus on perfecting the methods and tools while ignoring the question about the end we need to meet.

"The outcome should always determine the methods and tools."

Let's return to Batman and Commissioner Gordon again. Much like with testing, the ultimate purpose of both is to keep the city clean. The direct outcome though is much different. The police obey the law and try to make sure others do too. They monitor the traffic. Keep the streets safe by their presence. They do the occasional raid on the den of the bad guys, but only after getting a warrant from the judge, based on their detailed plans and the evidence at hand.

Batman, however, stays in the shadows. He does whatever it takes to smoke out the bad guys. He probably doesn't negotiate with the judge to approve his actions, but instead puts in all his skill and creativity to catch the bugs. Batman understands that no crook is the same and no battle plan survives the contact with the enemy.

To me, the first decision about testing is the balance between the two roles. How much of Gordon and how much of Batman do we need this time? Now, a testing professional might immediately catch the distinctions between the police and the Batman. But for others, we still have a lot of explaining to do to help them grasp all of the nuances. That is why I've developed a Storytool called *The Blueberry Parable*. So, let's leave Gotham and head into the woods.

First I've got to ask you this. Have you ever been to a forest to pick berries? This is an important question that will tie together all that we've thrown on the wall in this chapter.

Testing is the Sum Total of Two Activities

I love blueberry smoothies, so every August I spend a few weekends in the forest some 50 miles away from where I pick blueberries for the winter. I get cranky if I don't get my morning smoothie!

If I were a traditional testing professional making the trip, I would park my car by the side of the road, hop out and lay out the map on the hood. Then carefully plotting the route walking east from where the vehicle is parked, change direction and head north from a huge boulder that just can't be missed and finally I would reach a beautiful pond for a coffee break.

Now executing the plan gives a decent yield, and in the end, I'm a happy coffee drinker with a bucket full of berries. But what happens when I go home, put the berries in the freezer and head out again the next day? The plan was perfect yesterday, and I was satisfied with the results at the end of the first day, so I walk the same trail the following day. How many berries do you think I will get the second time?

There might be a spot that I missed the last time while taking selfies for Instagram. And there could be an area where the berries have ripened just enough to be picked. The third time starts to get frustrating because there are no berries in the bucket when I reach the pond for my coffee break. I might as well leave the bucket at home tomorrow.

But here comes the critical question of testing. What do I have as the outcome of my third trip? It's not berries, but I do have a bucket full of something. So what is it?

"Begin with the end in mind."

The outcome of my third trip, of course, is knowledge. I now have information that there are no berries left on this particular trail. In the domain of testing, this translates to a sense of certainty that everything still works as it always has done and that it matches our plan. After checking the trail, I get to assure my colleagues that everything still seems to be in place. This is an activity that I first learned to call checking from the testing coach and guru Michael Bolton. In the vibrator-phone project that I described earlier in the chapter, checking was the testing activity where we spend all of our scarce resources because that's how it had always been done. And because the organisation requires a 98% pass rate.

Only twice have I ever met testers with seemingly unlimited resources. They worked with critical aviation systems and high-end medical devices. I've never been in a project like that, so I've got no clue on how to spend unlimited testing resources. For the most part of this discussion though, it is safe to assume that your time for testing is minimal like mine. For us to find the most berries with the time that we have, what should we do on every single trip to the forest?

The answer is obvious. Creatively choosing new paths based on our extensive experience as berry pickers would be the way to achieve success. Going into the woods to get a sense of the environment and then on the new trail as we go along. This expedition-approach is the best way to get the best yield in the timeframe that we have. Getting the most berries in the bucket in other words.

Where checking aims at building confidence on the things that work, this other approach aims at revealing new places where our software might still break. This is an activity that I like to call hunting. Yes, there can be other related activities for testing too. Like demo sessions, meetings, planning or reporting. But, the easiest way to make sense of testing is to compress the idea into a single seed.

> "Testing is the sum total of two separate activities:
> Hunting and Checking."

The outcome of hunting is a bucket full of berries. Checking gives a bucket full of certainty. So which one do you need this time? Are you with Batman or Gordon?

This is the perfect moment to stop reading and do some thinking. Does your boss, colleague or the customer understand the two activities? If not, how could you plant the seed of this simple idea now to harvest a better crop tomorrow? Your answer to this question is paramount because...

> "Only with clarity of the outcome we desire, can we
> choose the methods and tools for our journey."

Most testing processes and tools that I've seen tend to lean towards checking. Checking is the easy way out. There are the test cases, metrics, and apps for doing all that. Checking feels like a controlled process with controlled outcomes and that is why it so tempting activity to choose for people who don't understand testing enough. The only problem is that a controlled process tends to produce expected outcomes. For example, Information that things still work the same or documentation which supports our assumptions. To reap the full benefit of professional testing, however, the team should focus on finding out the unexpected. Like finding a bucket full of bugs. Let's consider test cases for example.

Chapter 5

Mindset Mistake #2:

Cases Make Testing Better

Just out of curiosity, we did two test rounds with a team of consultants abroad. We split the group in two and gave different assignments to both of them. For the first assignment, the team was given a very clearly written test specification based on the product's requirements. We counted 18 bugs as an outcome of running 120 short test cases.

The second assignment we gave was only a short briefing. The mission was to test this product to your best knowledge and report all issues in a way you find best suited. We don't want any documents, only Jira tickets. As a result, we received 25 bug reports. In addition to that, the testing team (or the second half of it) got creative and used video capturing to demonstrate the bugs. The software developers also gave their thumbs up!

For the time spent in executing testing work, the result were 39% better when the testers put their focus on finding bugs and not following the test cases.

Yes. I know it was just a simple curiosity-driven experiment with lots of variables that we didn't take into account. But it was fun to play around with the possibilities.

Of course, this is common sense. It is obvious to most testers. We find more bugs by exploring than by repeating those recipes we call test cases. However, the phrase 'Common Sense' is a bit of a misnomer. Not all sense is common to everyone. Far from it!

Most of the test cases I still see today, try to describe in painstaking detail the steps needed to run the test. This is how you bake a double chocolate mud cake. These are the ingredients; this is the order you need to put them in the bowl; stir and cook in 180 degrees for 25 minutes. The expected result is a chocolatey delight.

> "Test cases tend to divert our effort and attention to
> entirely the wrong things considering our business."

The primary goal of a test case is not to describe HOW to run this specific test. That kind of recipe would be more suitable for a demo session for example. Or in a user manual for people who have no clue about how to use the software in the first place and don't have the guts to try it out. But regarding professional software testing, it ends up being annoying nitpicking with the details. It's easy to lose the big picture that way.

Instead of traditional chocolate cake recipes, professional testing could well do with only a short description of WHAT needs to get tested. To consider test cases as more of a checklist than a cookbook. In fact this approach has already been proved successful in industries aviation the safest form of transport in the world.

Testing Does it Backwards.

You know, I have a confession to make. I was afraid of flying when I was little. It might have something to do with my granny, who is still terrified, even though she will soon turn 100 years. The curious thing is that I became a software engineer and flying is an integral part of the job. Due to the initial fear of flying, I became obsessed with aeroplanes and the airline industry at an early age. Now I feel an incredible joy every time the plane takes off.

Flying has become one of the safest industries on earth, but this wasn't always the case. Boeing started to investigate the reasons behind fatal flight accidents in 1935 after U.S. Army Air Corps' Chief of Flight Testing Pete Hill and his crew were killed in a crash. It turned out that most of the accidents were the result of a series of human errors.

Major Hill was the most experienced and skilled pilot in the U.S. Army with over 18 years of experience. He was killed in a crash while flying the experimental Boeing Model 299 which was the prototype of the B-17 Flying Fortress Bomber. The investigation found that the crash had been caused by the ground crew leaving control surfaces in the locked position. It was not pilot error or a mechanical defect, so the investigators decided that more pilot training or experience was not the solution. What the team found out was painfully simple. An error by the ground crew had resulted in the deadly incident. As a result, a new approach was developed.

> "Skilful use of checklists can prevent most human errors."

This simple idea has been fully integrated throughout the flight industry today and is said to be one of the most important reasons why safety levels are so high. A surgeon and author, Atul Gawande explored the ideas even further in his remarkable book "The Checklist Manifesto." He successfully tested the concepts in clinical environments and saved thousands of lives in the process. Today, Dr. Gawande's approach is a standard that is used in a third of all operating theatres which has saved millions of lives worldwide.

What strikes me is the simplicity of the ideas behind checklists. We testers have used lists for ages in the form of classical test cases. The only problem is that the checklists we use are mainly recipes for trying to produce repeatable results. Much like a lousy cookbook. These "read-do" checklists rarely produce the results we desire the most. We may not have buckets full of berries, but we do have buckets full of certainty instead.

To me, one of the leading results of testing, is new relevant information about the product at hand. The data comes in the shape of bug reports for example. The more information we can produce at any given time, the better the efficiency. Designing, running and re-running these traditional read-do recipes is one of the biggest pitfalls for testers. It consumes a lot of time and produces minimal yield.

What Atul Gawande suggested in his book is that smart construction of "do-confirm" checklists would be the way to go in every industry. This kind of a list is a tool not to forget anything important. It's not a guide on how to run a test, but a reminder of what we want to get covered in the end.

Relating the "don't forget" information with just a sentence would be easy. In fact, Twitter proved that we can say most things with only 140 characters, although the limit today is up to 280. While even that wouldn't be necessary for real testing pros. Sometimes the most outstanding test results emerge from an empty sheet and creative thinking.

This shift of testing consciousness is a critical factor that eventually gives testers more freedom to explore. It is the ultimate source of new information, business-critical bug discoveries and even mental health in our line of duty.

This is not rocket science. Your management gains more bang for their buck when you can convince them to be brave and let testing professionals do the work the way they should be doing it.

The Power of Exceptions

Now, a test-case-believer could state that using cases isn't all bad. There still is a use for them. So the idea of checking and hunting does not apply in this specific environment. Well, I agree with you. As I wrote earlier, test cases are a great tool, but not for finding bugs. But before addressing the idea further, we need to zoom out for a moment.

Beliefs, doubts, critique and even boredom are defence mechanisms of the mind. To really make a lasting impact we need to learn to deal with the barrier of doubt before it deals with us. So, most of the ideas that I plan to plant in a team or organisation meet with this resistance. Without exception, I hear "what-if?" and "yeah-but" as excuses for why this new idea might not apply. So what can we do about it?

By far the best way to address these questions is to voice the doubts before the resistance takes its stand, and then explain why these doubts are warranted, but not applicable here. It is almost like mind reading to address doubts before anyone else voices the questions. This is the reason why I started the chapter by following the simple script.

1.   Voice out the doubt.

> "Yes. Now you might think that cases aren't all bad…"

2.   Agree with the doubt.

> "And you're right…"

3.   Debunking the doubt.

> "Test cases are a great tool, but not for finding bugs.
> Let me explain what they are for…"

Over the years I have helped software development in sectors like banking, refinery industry and even medical devices. In one such project the customer were developing a state of the art X-ray device that needed testing. Considering the radiation intensities they needed to make sure that the device matched the industry standards. In addition to that they needed to make sure that the device didn't kill anybody under any circumstances. In a project like this you need to invest heavily on producing evidence. If they were to face a situation ten years from now, where the X-ray tube they developed was thought to be the root cause for 1000 leukaemia incidents, they should be able to demonstrate with painstaking detail, how they did the tests and in which kind of conditions.

Similarly, a finance sector project might have a massive amount of laws and directives related to money flow and private information such as social security numbers or credit card information of customers. The GDPR act in Europe is one of the most recent changes in legislation today and products aiming for a market in Europe must conform to all of it. Without evidence about testing the product, the penalty for a simple incident could be as much as 4% of the total revenue of the company.

Test cases are an awesome tool for producing evidence of situations where we have a heavy burden of proof on our hands. This burden of proof might focus on questions like.

- Does the product meet the law or directives?

- Does the product meet the standards?

- Does the product meet our security promises?

- Does the product meet the contract that we have signed?

If you are in a position where it is vital to address questions like these, the outcome you would need is evidence and documentation that would withstand even an external audit. Write the test cases with the best of your skill and consider even using the ISO standard for test plan documents. In other words, do CHECKING.

Then, if you are in a position where there is no heavy burden of proof on your hands, ditch the checking activity or shrink it to an absolute minimum. It will only consume your limited time and resources in things that don't serve the outcome you need. The outcome you most likely need in this setting is to find the bugs before your user suffers as a result of them. In other words, do HUNTING.

Let me say it once more. Test cases are a great tool, but not for finding bugs. Test cases excel when you must create evidence to back up our contracts and legal requirements. But then you need to accept that the goal is to improve documentation, not to improve the product. But now we are left with one more question.

"Why can't we have check-cases and do some exploring while we are at it? Why can't we accomplish both goals in one fell swoop?"

And my answer is always - yes. You can do that too if you have extra time and resources on your hands. Human focus makes sure though, that it is inefficient to reach out for two contradictory outcomes at the same time.

The Contradiction

Tabby had found the half-finished manuscript in a trash can. She confronted Stephen after reading it through. She wanted to know the rest of the story.

"You've got something here," she said, "I really think you do."

So Stephen decided to give it a shot and finish the story about a schoolgirl called Carrie White. The book Carrie slowly gained momentum and launched the trajectory of the King family from a trailer park towards a brighter future. Today Stephen King is one of the most successful authors of our time.

Just recently I read Stephen King's autobiography. The book is called "On Writing" and it is a captivating story of how Stephen's career finally took flight after almost two decades of daily writing.

As a testing professional, I became inspired when I realised how writing is creative work, much like coding and bug hunting. As King himself put it, the creative process would never be able to work its magic if he had to put his focus on editing the text at the same time. No writer can create great stories while simultaneously trying to inspect the outcome for errors in the grammar, storyline or spelling. First comes the story, then comes the grooming.

As a professional bug hunter, I find this disturbing. We expect our coders to create beautiful software and amazing experiences for the users, but at the same time, we ask our coders to inspect their own work for bugs. We also expect our testers to use their creativity to find all possible situations where the software doesn't work, while at the same time, we need testers to script and execute test recipes we call cases.

Human attention is very limited. To demonstrate this, I invite you to try a brief experiment. Look around you right now. Stop and take 10 seconds to count how many red things you can find. If you were in a coffee shop, there might be red lights, red clothing, red accessories, red coffee cups and even something red to eat. Once you start to search for red things, you will most certainly find red things too. But now let me ask you. How many blue things did you find? You might recall a few, but most likely you didn't notice more. Human attention is extremely selective.

So now if you are looking for evidence that your software works. How likely is it, that at the same time you will find the places where it might break? Yes, you might find a few, but at the same time (I can't help but repeat myself), human attention is extremely selective. You will find mostly the things you consciously seek.

There is a contradiction to the work we do as software testing professionals. Usually the most significant results are the outcome of a creative process called hunting. We know this, and still, we try to mould the work of editing, into checking.

Editing and proofreading are phases that step in only after the writer has finished the creative work. So which one are you? The creator or the editor?

The terminology you use makes no difference here. Testing or quality assurance, is just a container for two very different activities with contradictory outcomes. Testers can do either - Checking or Hunting. So it all boils down to the decision we must make, a question we must answer weekly, daily or even hourly. Do we now need a bucket full of certainty or a bucket full of berries? Do we now need to build better evidence or a better product?

Chapter 6

Mindset Mistake #3:

Testing Comes After Development

The New World was first discovered and documented by the Europeans in 1497. An explorer by the name of John Cabot found North America. Just five years earlier Columbus had found his way to the Caribbean when looking for a sea route to India. The discovery heralded a new wave of sea travel across the Atlantic. The navigation methods used for crossing the seas were crude. There was no GPS back then and the methods were based on following the position of the stars and the Sun, combined with a magnetic compass. A ship would only reach the destination successfully if the heading were adjusted often enough using the observations made by the navigator. The steps were simple.

1. Observation and navigation

2. Aligning the heading accordingly

Even the Vikings knew this strategy almost a millennia prior to Columbus and his friends. Even before the vikings, around 3000 - 1000 BC, the Polynesians deployed the same principles in their voyages across the open Pacific Ocean. Their wayfinder tradition and knowledge was passed down the generations from master to apprentice in the form of songs and stories.

Despite all this ancient wisdom, we see modern software projects start with the bold assumption that we could plot the course just once at the beginning, write a foolproof agreement about it, and then hit the goal several years later. Time after time we get to read examples in the media, of projects that have lasted way too long, just to crash and burn at the end. To me it seems that there are two alternative routes to reach the goal in a project. Either you can navigate daily, or you can put your trust in blind luck.

The Aquatic Metaphors of the Software Industry

With so many aquatic metaphors floating around, we can easily drown under the waves! (Sorry, couldn't resist those!), but whether we consider navigation across oceans or the flow of a river, the nature of water as a dynamic element has the potential to take us on a journey. Depending on how we do it, we can either be the pilot or the passenger.

We often speak in terms of a stream of development. An ever changing river that we travel along to a mysterious destination. Sometimes the current pulls strongly and sends us through the white rapids, then there are the quiet pools where we can take a breath before diving into the current once more.

"Eventually we arrive at the ocean, ready to ship."

It is true that our software projects are exactly like riding the river. It is exhausting to paddle against the current. And at the same time the rocks under the surface always stay hidden until we hit them. The only problem with this mental image is that most of us attach it to a timeline. It is easy to consider a river with a beginning and an end. But at the same time we tend to miss the more important point.

You see, all too frequently I meet people who see testing as a downstream activity. They see testing as something that happens after the development is done. By the time you've reached the mouth of the river, it is too late to watch out for the hidden rocks, whirlpools and falls.

It is true that a few decades ago, testing might have been a pre-release activity. The last hurdle to jump before shipping. But is it really any different today? Now we talk about agile software development and sprinting.

Let me give you an example. David is a modern day developer. He is hammering code in a project with Clara the Coder. A Sprint of two weeks has been rolling at a fast pace and the final days took a lot of overtime. When the team finished their work, the software gets sent to Tina the Tester.

Testing in this setting is often found at the end of development cycles, or even at the end of each multi-week sprint. We've learned to shift testing upstream and it's not a bad idea. But at the same time it is an error in the mindset no matter how well it was disguised. It's still not agile to me. A closer look often reveals that it is an incremental or iterative way of creating software. Developers withdraw into their chambers to work on the epics, stories, and tasks for the sprint and once finished, they deliver the software for testing.

> "Suddenly, work that claims to be Agile seems quite
> like a series of small waterfalls."

Incremental software development is not automatically Agile even though we might insist on using the term. Agile, on the other hand, might be incremental as well.

Testing is not a downstream floodgate before shipping. As long as we deploy testing in this miniature series of waterfalls, we fall short of its full potential. What we should do with our metaphors is simple.

> "We need to place testing inside our raft with all of
> the developers and row like hell."

So now we are left with a question. What then, makes testing agile?

How Testing Helps us Develop Faster?

Today it seems to be all about speed. We talk about time-to-market. We try to measure efficiency as a factor of time. We automate all we can. Agility is more and more about fast response times to the ever changing demands of the market or the client. But, let me ask you a question. Do you still remember learning a second language back in the day?

I spent my elementary school years in a small yellow wooden schoolhouse with only 100 other pupils. Growing up in this idyllic environment makes me a small town boy, you might say.

During the third grade, we started learning our first foreign language. For most Finns it was of course, English. In our first session, we came up with English names for us. I was "Andy." My friend Aki was a big fan of the TV series "Jake and the Fatman", so he wanted to be "Jake".

Those early language lessons always started with the vocabulary. Building a library of concepts and meaning is a natural first step in learning any language. Then, pretty soon we would move on to creating phrases based on the newly learned vocabulary and finally experiment in pairs with some dialogue.

"Hi! My name is Andy." I said.

"Hi! Andy, I'm Jake" Aki replied.

Through dialogue like this, we learn quickly because we instantly receive feedback from our partner.

So what if we moved this exercise into a software project? Calvin the coder builds a new feature. He makes the change and the number of lines could grow from hundreds to even thousands. Finally he commits it to the version control. It's just like voicing his line of the dialogue.

"Hi! I'm Calvin"

A sprint passes. Or even a month in a more classic setting. Then a tester takes the changes in for some testing and a few bug reports emerge on Jira. Finally, weeks after the actual coding, Calvin gets the response he has been waiting for. If it were the elementary school exercise, he would finally hear-

"Hi, Calvin! I'm Tina"

By the time he gets the response, Calvin has probably already forgotten the whole dialogue. If we consider this setting as a learning environment, who would benefit from such an extensive time-lag in the discussion?

In coding, the question would be whether Calvin can remember what kind of changes he worked on so long ago? What were the dependencies inside those software components? What lines and files of source code did he touch back then? Digging through old lines of code will take time and making changes causes a growing risk of breaking dependencies too.

> "It's like digging through a box of old family photos
> and not being sure what to look for."

Can you remember what you did two weeks ago at this time? Or a month ago? I don't, and neither do most of the developers.

Digging into the human memory has an implication. Recalling and reworking what we did weeks ago takes a lot of time. Time which could be better spent building new things, while at the same time, the risk of mistakes we call regression grows as well. This is a problem which seems to systematically plague projects when the development cycle is long and where testing only steps in downstream. I've noticed that there are two options to reduce the risk of delays and after-shipment regression.

1. Speed up the dialog between testing and development.

Or

2. Pre-budget plenty of time to fix things and hope for the best.

It's an easy choice when you're faced with these options, Isn't it?

A flowing dialogue between developer and tester will produce the results you seek. This leads to faster development with fewer bugs. Now looking back to the series of small waterfalls that some might call "kinda agile". In that setting, the feedback is not fast. Dialogue does not flow if the team works in cycles of development followed by testing followed by development followed by testing. In this scenario, the question is not about teamwork, but instead, the cooperation of two teams.

I admit it's a line in the sand to claim a definition for agile testing. But to me, it's not a single characteristic of the testing routine. It's the direction in which the testing process evolves. Move up stream, get ever closer to the development and make the feedback loop a bit smaller every day. Move from gatekeeping the production releases closer to testing the outcomes of every sprint; towards testing the epics, stories and finally, testing every task at the time of development.

Nothing in life stays static. Besides, hardcoding values is dangerous. Everything evolves or erodes, and so it is with your testing. But can you tell if you are heading towards or away from the development?

Creating a Tool From a Story

There are a handful of people who still consider testing to be the last acceptance gateway before shipping. Luckily for us, their numbers are declining every year. It has a direction too it seems. For me, meeting with people who see testing as the downstream activity, the story of learning a new language has made an impact on many occasions. It's been a useful tool. The impact might not be visible immediately, but given time, it too grows into a fruitful change in the testing culture.

These kind of a stories work for a reason. Most people have a personal experience about learning a new language that they can either share or relate to. Those shared or sometimes even imagined experiences become the common ground that we can use for planting the seeds of new ideas. And what makes it even more powerful is the introductory question. Can you remember exactly what you did on this day two weeks ago? Most people have no clue about it.

Although, I do have one exception to share with you. In one testing workshop, an attendee said that he had been to the dentist on this specific Thursday two weeks ago at 9.35. Root canal therapy wasn't his favourite treatments and besides he already had a phobia for dentists. Here is another example. Can you tell what did on September the 11th 2001? That's when the whole world held its breath watching the news about the World Trade Center in New York. Most people I know remember in bright detail what they were doing at the time.

Memory does work in high detail but it requires emotionally engaging moments. Most of our day to day activity is not that exciting, so memory fades away fast. Having discussed the mechanics of memory, we now have a shared experience that we can use to build new ideas upon. That is the shared belief. The "Why" which we can use to build more. With this kind of base, it becomes easier to convey an idea such as seeing testing as an integral part of the everyday development practice and not simply a floodgate down the stream. The following are the four principles that I have used in creating tools out of stories. Similar structures can be discovered in more detail in books like Pitch Anything by Oren Klaff or TED Talks by Chris Anderson.

1. Make it personally and emotionally engaging to the audience you have. By this I mean clients, colleagues and bosses!

2. Call on the mental images and the experiences of your audience to establish your common ground.

3. Use metaphors, examples and references to demonstrate the core principle behind your idea. At the same time keep the idea in your back pocket for a little longer.

4. Finally you must draw out the idea by connecting the ideas with a question "So, what can we learn from this?" for example. This plants the actual seed of your idea with tools such as questions or even a twitter-friendly headline (Explain your idea in 140 or 280 characters). The hard part is usually forgotten. Mindsets do not change quickly. You need to nurture the seeds of ideas with patience. It will take time to grow.

Now let's deploy these four ideas on the same mindset mistake we started with. Testing is a downstream activity. For someone familiar or even enthusiastic about motor sports, the following story has the potential to transform your thinking. On the other hand for someone who feels disconnected from sports of any kind, there most likely is nothing to be gained from this example. So understanding the audience is intensely important.

Stars of the Development Team

Imagine a rally car race. The car is tearing along the snaking mountain roads at 130kph, the driver and co-driver are staring death in the eye. Ravines on one side of the road, a solid rock wall on the other. The driver is the star who is responsible for getting to the finish line safely in 1st place. Then we have the co-driver. He sits in the passenger seat and reads the pace notes, calmly communicating them to the driver. There is little emotion in his voice. Just clear concise information about the next few corners. Nothing more. Dialogue and cooperation is the only way to succeed in rallying.

Now, let's consider the music industry. I'm a huge fan of Bruce Dickinson. To me he is an amazing singer and entrepreneur. He's had a formidable career with Iron Maiden and as a solo artist. He is also a commercial airline pilot -

just for a hobby, and often pilots the tour plane for Iron Maiden world tours. Bruce is clearly the star of the show, but he would not be able to make it without the rest of the band, an incredible team of assistants, techies and roadies.

I've got some news for you. I'm a tester and I'm not the Bruce Dickinson of this team. The odds are that you aren't either. I've met way too many testers who act in an assertive way and keep on pushing the developers with the bugs they find. They act as if testers are the stars of the show and it ends up annoying everybody.

How good a job would the co-driver do in a rally if he waited at the finish line to inform the driver of the route he needed to take? I bet no team would win a single race with such a mindset. How good a job would a sound or lighting engineer do in a rock concert by only showing up backstage after the show to inspect the rig and do the sound check? I bet no band would break through with such a mindset. So why is it that we expect testing to be the ultimate roadie or co-driver while at the same time only appearing at the last moment before this amazing product leaves our hands?

The tester is not the star of the show. Instead, the tester makes sure that the stars can shine even brighter.

Chapter 7

Mindset Mistake #4:

The Software is Not Ready for Testing

Baked overnight, fresh-from-the-oven, the latest software version is on your desk. A good tester ploughs through 100 cases a day, maintaining a steady pace until the test set is done. That kind of a tester isn't very talkative and doesn't ask inconvenient questions. That is the hallmark of a good tester. Or is it?

Of course, a skilled testing professional challenges the implementation of the product. Most of the time, however, a professional tester is not interested in proving that the product works. In reality, a professional is more interested in where the product might still break. Where is the next bug that could ruin our business, hiding?

This kind of curiosity is something that is not turned on or off on demand. Way before challenging the implementation, a truly skilled testing professional has already challenged the architecture of the product. The tester is interested in questions such as - how many users can we expect on the first day of launch? What kind of load balancer is our service using? Are there legal reasons why we should double down on our security plan?

You will find, that with these questions, the professional is already testing the product. Gathering information before doing the testing doesn't really differ from doing the testing. It's only a different part of the whole thing that we test.

But even before the first discussion with the architect, a truly skilled testing guru has already begun challenging the concept of the product. The tester is interested in questions like - where does the money comes from, and why? Who will be the first to buy this and how? The professional begins to test the product in the first conversation with the product's owner, and maybe even with the end user.

Once more you will find, that with these questions, the professional is already testing the product. Gathering information prior to doing the testing doesn't really differ from doing the testing. It's only a different part of the whole product that we test.

Given what we know about testing, I've got to pose yet another question. When is the software mature enough for testing? Testing, by nature, is challenging, as is questioning the product. So at which specific point in time should we start doing it? And how much of it is enough?

I ended up pondering this after a morning of vomiting.

How Much is Enough?

The dimly glowing clock face showed 3:35 am. I woke up with an exploding headache. The toilet light cut my eyes, and a cold sweat was pouring down my forehead. I had the sensation of vertigo from a headache as I was throwing up.

I was in a hotel room in London. This time the traditional hangover wasn't the cause though. The seminar day had spanned an intensive period of 15 hours straight, and I had forgotten to drink my morning coffee. A combination of dehydration and caffeine withdrawal tends to spark a fierce headache. This one was the worst by far.

Luckily my headache attacks are curable with stimulants and painkillers. I got through the night by mixing a double dose of instant coffee into the cold tap water. It tasted terrible, but on the other hand, it did its job, along with 800mg of painkillers. In the morning I had to continue medicating the condition further to get back in shape. Later I wondered how messed up I was. Having to drink coffee to be able to sleep is something that I would call an addiction.

My medication strategy for a headache is simple. One painkiller tablet and a cup of coffee always does the job. Doubling the tabs and the cups of coffee makes me feel better, faster. Usually by the third dose, the headache has gone. However, the following morning, while sitting and eating the hotel breakfast, I started to think. How much medication is enough? If I started the day with 7x400mg of my chosen painkiller, and two pints of coffee, I'd probably feel even worse. Superfoods, painkillers, stimulants, alcohol, fitness, resting and even testing become detrimental when taken in excessive amounts.

Most things in life follow a diagram where the horizontal axis describes the dosage and the vertical axis demonstrates the benefit. When increasing the amount, the benefit increases accordingly. Upping the input gives more of the outcome until at some point, it doesn't anymore. We hit a plateau of benefits, and then the benefits start to act against themselves. The shape of the curve resembles an inverted U. This graph stands true for nearly all kinds of activity. In economics, it's called the law of diminishing returns. In the domain of software testing, some of the common questions are: When should we start? How much should we invest? Maybe we could start tomorrow? When have we tested enough? On every occasion we could guess the optimal investment, but then most of our success would be based on luck.

Think about Ben the Project Leader for example. "A splendid idea!" Ben explains in the project planning meeting. "It is without doubt a sensible idea to divide the development budget in a way that testing can be bought as a service only when we need it." His plan is to run the first testing round for the release candidate number one. After getting the results, the team will fix the bugs, and the second round will be used to verify that everything went as planned. Two rounds of testing are just perfect! A surprising number of software projects use Ben's style. The approach is ultra sensible as long as we assume that:

1. We do not design any new use cases, requirements or stories.

2. The product does not change anymore. It's frozen.

3. The bug fixes do not break anything else.

In projects like this, it is inevitable that the scheduling fails when we introduce testing. The original plan just happened to be unrealistic. Professional testing done too late discovers more bugs than expected. Much more. Always. Then the deadlines become unreachable because fixing that amount of bugs takes an unexpected amount of time. Usually, on the first testing round, we also come up with test ideas that we cannot execute. Some of the bugs prevent us from reliably testing the very functionality they infest.

During the verification round, we again discover loads of new bugs just because the testers now know the product better, and because some fixes let us act on our previous testing ideas. Of course, the probability of flawless bug fixing without any regression is next to nothing as well. Ben's plan is great if the quality of our product is already of exceptional quality. For every regular project, however, it just won't work. Testing too late will destroy those deadlines.

While trusting in fate might be a great idea when playing the lottery, it's not the smartest move in professional life. Instead of Lady Luck, my recommendation is to instead aim for the first meaningful dose and do it fast. The smallest impactful investment is discovered by starting from the beginning of the U curve and tuning it up with experience and learning.

So the simple answers could look like this:

When should we start testing?

> Right now.

How much should we invest in testing?

> Invest a little at first. See if a single day provides you any benefit. Then invest more if the gains present themselves.

When have we tested enough?

> When the returns start diminishing.

When is the software mature enough for testing?

> If you build software for this decade, the software is never mature enough. Eventually you've got to start and it might as well be right now.

Maybe we should start tomorrow?

> You could. But please refer to the previous chapter first: Mindset Mistake #2: Testing is Done after the Development

Three Levels of Testing

I once sat in a meeting with a video streaming service provider. They were starting a project to develop the next generation of their backend. An uncomfortable silence fell over the meeting room after one question.

A colleague of mine by the nickname Tuna had just taken a long sip of coffee before breaking in with the question. "As a tester, my job is sometimes to ask silly questions. Which load balancer were you planning on using for this project?" Tuna has an amazing way to prime his questions with a disarming tone and explaining his role as just-a-tester. "So can we handle the traffic when the marketing campaign launches?" He continued.

It seems that beyond the horizon of everyday work, there is something only a few remember or dare to question. The non-functional areas of the software that we develop, such as security and performance that play a central role in building an outstanding web service and still, we rarely discuss concrete actions to deal with them. "I thought the service provider takes care of the traffic!?" is a typical answer.

In development, we add new features to the product we are building. We split epics into stories and then into tasks. And it is easy to do with visible functionality. The non-functional aspects like security and performance are built-in to the product, and they are characteristics of well-designed architecture. But they are hard to consider in the daily trenches of development efforts.

Outstanding products are a combination of awesome add-on features and high quality built-in characteristics. Despite this, the responsibility of the built-in characteristics almost always remains in the grey zone. We need a magical someone to take ownership for asking the hard questions and let the uncomfortable silence hang like a rain cloud over the meeting room.

Here are a few examples that Tuna uses to explain the immediate impact of the non-functional characteristics. Poor performance decreases the cash flow right now.

1. Every 100-millisecond optimisation in online store performance raises the revenue by 1%. It means money!

2. On the other hand, every 100ms of lag decreases the revenue by 1%. [7]

3. 53% of mobile site visitors will leave a page that takes longer than three-seconds to load. Think about the attention span of a consumer!

4. Sites that load within five-seconds see an increase of 70% in average sessions times.[8]

5. Google indexing punishes you for slow performance? So most people won't even find you in the first place!

I believe that there is nothing to argue about here. It makes no difference what your role is. If you want to protect and build the business you serve, take ownership of both the added-on features and built-in characteristics. Learn to ask the inconvenient questions while things are still easy and fast to fix.

Dare to Ask the Difficult Questions.

The chief of marketing was the first to break the silence in the meeting room. "Why is the load balancer so important?" she asked. Tuna replied, with the impassioned tone of a professional "Well. In my experience with these two quite common load balancers, there will be huge scalability issues with video streaming". I watched the conversation unfold with amazement. We had discovered and fixed a truly expensive bug way before a single line of code had been written.

Regarding software maturity and timing of testing, I feel the need to point it out one more time. Testing is so much more than just challenging the

____

[7] Reported by both Amazon and Walmart

[8] Reported by Google

implementation. I like to illustrate this with three levels of development where testing should be involved. Let's call it the triad of testing.

1. Testing challenges the concept

2. Testing challenges the architecture

3. Testing challenges the implementation

The earlier we engage, the faster and cheaper it is to fix the mistakes. So to me, every tester should be a part of all three levels of the triad. The only problem, however, is that testers rarely get invited to meetings about architecture let alone the business concepts. That is why I say the triad is a ladder that we need to learn to climb. We as testers must earn our way to upper levels. But before we continue, I must warn you. There is a risk to this idea.

The Tripwire of Challenging

A friend of mine had just accepted a job offer from a well respected development company in Helsinki. Just a few months earlier he had taken the amazing Rapid Software Testing course to take his expertise to a totally new level. With a mindset of hunting the bugs before a single line of code was written he took on the new job. It was such a blast to put his newly acquired skills to work. Going around challenging colleagues, clients and superiors was beneficial for the business and it was fun too!

Six months into the work, on one Friday morning he got an SMS from the head of department asking him to join for a brief morning meeting. "Now that's odd" my friend thought, but went along to the meeting. In the executive room there were three people waiting for him. The boss, the company lawyer and the employee trustee. In that meeting my friend got a written warning for bullying coworkers at the office. And it was true he later said to me, that he had noticed that most of the colleagues avoided him in the coffee room and during lunch breaks too.

As it turned out, a tester who is too eager to show off these skills is prone to trip terribly on the social construct of the team. No one wants to work with an annoying smart-arse. Development work in any setting is challenging enough as it is. Despite the obvious benefits of someone testing and finding bugs from the architecture or even the concept earlier, emotions steer behaviour. A real testing guru knows this and because of that, they constantly practice their skills of communication, influence and human connection. We like to call these the "soft skills" of our profession. But it's just like the author and guru, Seth Godin puts it.

> We give too little respect to the skills when we call them "soft" and imply that they're optional. Culture defeats strategy, every time.
>
> -Seth Godin

I have noticed that there are two ways to deploy this "triad of testing". You either find a team filled with masochists who would welcome annoying smart-asses who challenge everything, or you must do it through stealthy means. The test guru who nourishes the culture instead of being the smart-ass, gets invited to all the relevant meetings because to others, it seems like a smart idea.

Testers always start at the bottom of the triad in order to prove themselves. Only then can they start working their way up the ladder. It takes time and practice, but it will happen.

Habits and Beliefs of an Outstanding Professional

I think that there are two key factors that define success in both our professional and personal lives. That is why I like this question.

> "What are the habits and beliefs of highly successful people?"

I have a massively successful colleague who works as a tester on a financial sector project. They develop a state of the art invoicing platform for the future of the smartest electricity companies. The colleague of mine has an above average reputation. This is reflected in the calls from both clients and headhunters who ask for his services on a daily basis. He doesn't answer the phone anymore.

Though this is not a story about project management, let me share some background first. His current project is sophisticated because they have a testing team of three engineers for ten developers. A ratio that I haven't seen too often. Needles to say, their product is exceptionally good. At the time of writing this, the latest software release has been undergoing the finishing touches for a few weeks now, and it is meant to be released next week. My colleague knows that the software has three critical bugs in it, which he has already reported to the developers two weeks ago. The bugs, for some reason, have still not been taken up to be fixed yet.

My tester friend is a smart guy. He has made sure to become friends with the developer in charge. He even set up his laptop across the aisle to this lead developer. "I occasionally whisper things like, this is what the bug looks like, to my developer friends," he said to me once. Even though three critical bugs are still not fixed, the tester has not escalated the subject up the chain of command, so I had to ask him why? "Well, I trust my guys and gals. I trust them to fix these issues before the release, and my job is to help them succeed" he told me.

Because this specific tester is a great guy and is liked by the developers for his style, the team always takes his word seriously. Because of this he faces the classic argument only once or twice a year, typically with someone new on the team.

"It's not a bug. It's a feature."

With patience and a subtle approach he makes sure that the team understands why the bugs he finds are relevant, and that the team fixes them before the release. And miraculously, the bugs seem to disappear just before release date. I've seen it happen many times over the years.

"How do you work that magic then? How is it that you get so much better results than most of your colleagues?" I asked him. "Well, it all boils down to three beliefs that I focus on daily," he replied. "I believe that above all else I am a customer servant. I am here to serve these people so that they can make killer apps and products. We are on the same side."

"I believe that sharing all the credit with my team builds trust. And I think that taking all the blame does the same. Trust is my biggest asset because the more I have, the less I need to defend the relevance of my results. By the first two habits I am building a professional reputation. First it happened within my team, then within my office and finally, it seems like our offices abroad have started to call me for advice too." My friend concluded.

These ideas have nothing to do with the vocational testing skill or the title my friend has, but to me, it seems clear that this is leadership at its core. It's no wonder he has built up such a reputation.

Culture Defeats Tactics Every Time.

A testing guru is someone who understands that soft skills are real skills. This ladder of challenging the implementation, the architecture and the concept needs to be worked again and again with every new team deploying our service. Wearing that white belt with every new project and working up to the black belt.

Challenging the concept and the architecture are the ninja skills of a tester. When used with wisdom, nobody even notices it happening. Everything simply seems to fall in its place naturally. But now if we get back to the original question. In which situation is the software "not mature" enough for testing? The only situation I can come up with is one where the organisation does not understand the benefit of testing before coding. And the only situation where this can happen is where the organisation culture does not yet embrace the full benefit of testing. So is it our software or our culture that isn't mature enough for early testing?

And we already know what to do with a broken culture. All of the change, hides inside seeds of ideas that we must learn to plant and feed.

Chapter 8

Mindset Mistake #5:

We Need Workload Estimates

There is a fantastic restaurant called Istanbul near where I live. They have the Chaîne des Rôtisseurs plaque on the door. Everything inside is a reflection of excellence, and their Tripadvisor rating is top notch.

One of their most popular dishes is a juicy lamb fillet fried on an open fire served with creamy caper sauce. A friend of mine was coming over from London, and I suggested we'd try the famous lamb. "I'm not a huge fan of lamb" my friend admitted after a discussion "so how does it taste?"

Of course, explaining it makes no difference. There is no way to know how this famous open-fired lamb tasted unless we ate the famous open-fired lamb first. You cannot truly know something before you've experienced it.

The next day at work my client asked the same question. How can we know how long it will take to test our new release candidate? Could you give us a workload estimate? "The thing is, that you cannot know something unless you've experienced it first. There is no way to know how the Lamb of Istanbul tasted unless you ate the Lamb of Istanbul first" I explained to the client "It's the same with software too..."

I have no way to know the quality of the software when it arrives on my desk. I only know after I've tested it. And guess what? The quality of the software is the defining factor on how fast or slow it is to test. It's slow to work with bad software and fast to work with good. So which is it? We have no way to know that without testing the software first.

The thing with testing is that it will always fill up the time we allow it. Give me one hour of time, and I will fill it up with testing. Give me a day, and I will fill it up with testing. Give me a week, and I will fill that with testing too. After an extensive monologue, I finally asked the client "So considering our budget, resources and planned schedule, how much time do we have? How much will you give me?"

She gave me three days.

A Test Case is Like a Suitcase

Another common way to frame the same topic is to hide it inside the concept of test cases. I've met with loads of managers who insist on how many test cases we should design to be able to test this software. Most testing professionals face that question or variations of it on a regular basis. The question about the number of test cases can basically be reduced to the underlying reason of estimating workload or measuring progress. In fact, most seemingly strange questions we testers face, can actually be reduced to one of the mindset mistakes described in this book.

But let me give you an example about this one. When faced with the question of counting or guessing test cases, my strategy is simple. I could test your software with just one test case. And the case does not even need to be complicated. Consider Twitter for example. To demonstrate the idea, I just planned a test case for them.

Step 1: Test Twitter.com

Expected result 1: Twitter.com works

Nothing mysterious there. With this remarkable test case, you get a requirement coverage of 100% and equally impressive test coverage too. With this one case, we can also measure the system's functionality reliably. Right?

Any project leader with some basic knowledge of testing would of course find my logic faulty. "You just cannot estimate any system with one test case. You don't even get any metrics from that" they would say. Ok. So if my one case isn't enough, how many would you like to have? What if we doubled the resolution of our test plan? What if we split that one case into two; one for the front end and one for the back end. Would that be enough?

How many times should we double the amount of cases to get "good" metrics? What would be a high enough resolution for your expectation? Should we design 10, 100, 1000 or 10,000 test cases?

I don't know the answer for Twitter. I don't even have an idea about the scale. 1000 cases might be just as correct as 10,000. And I'm pretty sure that the project leader doesn't know the answer either. The whole conversation will be based on our biased assumptions.

You can try this out for yourself. Write a test case like the one above. You can choose the target freely. Then start doubling the resolution. Split each test case into two new ones and see how far you can get before you start to get frustrated. I bet you didn't even get to FullHD here.

The number of test cases is an arbitrary figure. It's subjective. And this exercise is a tool for you to demonstrate it to others as well. So, a test case is like a suitcase. You never know what's inside.

Using test cases in estimating workload or measuring progress is arbitrary because we have no way to know the extent of each case or the depth of our interpretation. It's the same issue all over again as with the Lamb of Istanbul. A similar monologue applies to guessing cases too. "So considering our budget, resources and planned schedule, how many cases would satisfy or need for numbers? How much time will you give me?"

Now of course I admit that with experience, we all get better at guessing. And guessing is not a bad thing. I do have a rule of thumb for taking a leap of faith as well. When asked to guess, I always make sure every party knows it is guessing that we are doing now. After making sure of that, my guess is always the same. Invest 20% of your total time in testing.

A Script to Dealing with Estimates

The question about workload estimates is actually so common that for this one I've developed a simple script to follow. Countless times it has proven itself. See for yourself.

Step 1. Always be willing to help:

Most testers tend to start by saying things like "how would I know?"or "It kinda depends." Some even toss a few numbers like 2 or 6 in the air. 2 or 6 of what? Hours, days or weeks? This approach hardly helps anybody.

Instead of being confrontational, we need to align ourselves side by side, and all looking in the same direction before moving forward together. So the first step is to accept instead of deny. Here's an example of how I start: "I understand that we need an estimate to be able to plan the project going forward…"

Step 2. Use the AND -principle:

Most testers tend to communicate with a BUT-principle. Let me give you an example. "I agree with you on this BUT, I think that…"

You see, the simple use of the word "but" essentially negates the whole sentence that came before it. In principle it means that I'm only saying I agree with you, but in fact I don't really agree with you at all. Here is how I do it instead: "…AND at the same time, we know that the speed of testing depends on the quality of the software…"

Step 3. Deploy your Storytool:

Mine is the one with the favourite dish from a local restaurant. You can steal that one or come up with your own. Here is how I do it: "…This is what I mean. There is a fantastic restaurant near the place I live. It's called The Istanbul…"

Step 4. Explain the principle:

In testing, quality is the defining factor of speed. Here's how I conclude: "… Because we have no way to know the quality before we test, estimating is impossible. A better question is, how much time do we have in the context of our project budget and schedule?"

The Script:

1. "So I understand what you need and why…"

2. "…AND at the same time we need to admit that…"

3. "…We have no way to know how the Lamb of Istanbul tasted unless we ate it first…"

4. "…What I mean is that we have no way to know the quality of the software before we have tested it. And the speed of testing mostly depends on the current quality of our software."

A workload estimate in reality is an agreement for spending our precious resources. So a more important question is always - How much time do we have? After agreeing that, my job as the professional is to know how to use the time that we have for optimal results. But how on earth would quality define our speed?

Read on. It has everything to do with the concept of coverage.

Chapter 9
Mindset Mistake #6:

Coverage is a Result of Efficiency

"Hello boys and girls and welcome to the meeting! How many test cases did you run this week? How many could you have squeezed in if you really tried?"

I remember it like it was yesterday—our test manager asking the question. Not more than a decade ago I was still involved in software projects that went by the V model. For every result we delivered, there needed to be a corresponding plan and an evidence document as well. We had solved a part of the dilemma by deploying the HP Test Director in our project, and we had a total of 2500 test cases and counting. A typical day for a tester consisted of running 78 test cases on average. The standard day of our manager consisted of building reports about progress and figuring out how to improve the throughput of our team.

What was interesting about the situation was how evident it was to see testing as an assembly line. Just like in a factory full of monkeys executing test cases as efficiently as possible. The monitoring solutions in our test management tool were just priceless. Failing to meet a minimum coverage of 50 cases in a day, would cause our manager to storm in, asking how he could be of assistance.

We measured the speed of testing as the function of test cases ran in an hour. That was actually one of our key performance indicators in the project. If the hourly coverage faltered even a bit, that was interpreted as inefficiency.

Being the young tester that I was, I was still certain there was something fishy going on in thinking this way. It was all messed up, but our project manager accidentally said it in one meeting and I jotted it down in my little black book of testing.

> "Coverage is a function of efficiency."

Now, years later, having come to terms with this frustrating experience, I could not disagree more. I lacked the tools and the courage to explain my idea to others. Instead I complied and at the same time resolved not to subject myself to madness like this again.

The mindset mistake might be obvious to a tester, but it escapes those who attempt to lead testing as an industrial process. Let me explain.

What Happens when a Tester Paints the Beach House?

We call it "the Villa". In reality, it's more of a hut 60km north from where I live. It's our summer place, where we regularly spend our vacations. I go there to write from time to time as well. There is a small beach-house-sauna built close to the shore and every night we warm it up.

Not long ago we decided that the sauna needed painting. It's on the shore after all and at the mercy of the weather. New paint would give the building some protection from the occasional storms that pass through.

One Friday afternoon I left the office early to go to the hardware store and buy all the equipment we would need for the job. We needed at least two shades of paint. One for the walls and one for the window frames. Then brushes, of course, and a massive roll of plastic and some tape to cover the terrace and windowsills.

Then we hit the road and arrived at our cottage just as the weather fairy decided to turn the wind up all the way to eleven. So we had to wait for the morning to start the work. Waking up early, the team of diligent helpers made sure the protective plastics were taped where needed, and by afternoon we finally got to work.

We applied two layers of paint to the small beach house before sundown. In the morning we deconstructed our protective plastics and the ladder system. Finally, we took care of the finishing touches detailing the window frames with small brushes. Our weekend was a success.

Afterwards we sat down around the table eating the traditional salmon soup with a few beers. Looking back on the job, it was evident that we spent only a few hours of our time doing the actual painting. In other words - coverage. We spent most of our time gathering the right equipment, setting up the protective plastic and waiting for the paint to dry. Finally, we put our effort into investigating the details and doing the nitpicking part of the work.

No matter where we go, most of our time is not spent on the actual task that we set out to do. Instead, we do a considerable amount of setup before getting on with the work and a fair amount of cleanup and investigation too.

To explain the time allocation, I use a simple SCI model that I took away from my first RST course years back. For me, it is easy to remember the model by the association with the TV series Crime Scene Investigators Miami, David Caruso and his famous sunglasses. "Heeeyyyaaaah!!!"

Even though in my memory anchor the letters are all mixed CSI or SCI, it doesn't make much difference. The main thing is that the letters are there.

Each one represents a base activity of a typical testing session. But before I explain each of them, I must say it once more. This model has proven to be one of the most valuable testing tools I have.

S stands for Setup.

In software testing, this activity tends to be stuff like setting up the test data, rigging the database and the servers, gathering release notes or maybe deploying the build into the test environment. In addition, I've noticed that something unexpected always happens that expands the proportion of this activity. The unit test framework might have broken down during the night or my password was locked due to some strange mess-up at the IT department of the company. Setup is everything that we need to take care of before we get to start testing.

C stands for Coverage.

In testing terms, this is the activity where I constantly move forward to test new areas of the software. For example I might open the login page. Everything there seems to be in place. All the positive and negative scenarios I can come up with seem to work fluently and no bugs intervene. Then I proceed to the main view of our testing target and so on. It's basically the activity where I brush the paint on our beach house-sauna. If I was a coder, I might even substitute the C here for Coding, This is the actual work that would have been visible in our Test Director all those years ago as well.

I stands for Investigation.

When I find a bug, I must pause with my progress. "What just happened there?" I might ask. Capturing screenshots, taking notes and finally working my way to Jira to report the ticket is all about the investigation activity. I've noticed, that here too, something unexpected always happens that expands the proportion of this activity. Like last month I noticed a colleague wrestling with a stupid issue. The VPN access to the customer's ticketing system had expired and it took a full 24 hours to wait for the access to be renewed. After a lot of unnecessary setup we finally got our bug reports in.

The scenario plays out in most of the projects we have. It is a surprisingly thin slice of time that we genuinely spend on the coverage activity. If we mostly focus on setting the rig up (S) or capturing and reporting bugs (I), then the focus is away from gaining coverage (C). Setup and Investigation consume a bunch of time, not to mention all the other pointless activities such as meetings, planning and documentation, headhunter calls or occasional sick leave.

> Gaining coverage is not a function of efficiency. It's
> always a function of Focus.

It is mostly about how many hurdles less we need to hop over in every other area of our projects. All of the focus in Setup activities is focus away from Coverage. All of the focus in Investigation activities is focus away from Coverage. You get the drill. Now think about your next meeting. How does that contribute to the coverage you gain today? To make the idea applicable, we are left with just one question.

What could you do this week to decrease the time that you spend in Setup and Investigation or any other distraction?

Think testability, think dev-ops, think turning off your phone and email notifications, think automation, think outside of the box.

Fitness Tracker of your Test Session

The question dropped by our manager back in the V-model-days still haunts me, although, these days I know how to deal with it in discussions. How many tests could you squeeze in if you really tried? Or there is another typical version of it too.

> "Why haven't you tested more? Is this all you've
> got?!?"

I've noticed that there is a simple and highly efficient tool to back up the idea of a painted beach house-sauna. Something that is hard to argue with. I love the concept of high intensity interval training and I have a few fun apps such as HIIT timers that I use in testing. In essence you can setup the timer to beep on a regular interval be it 30 seconds or 15 minutes.

Occasionally I do a testing session with my HIIT timer set on 10 minute intervals. In addition to that I have a SCI tally at the side of my session journal. Every time I hear a beep from the timer, I take note on the tally about which activity was dominant during the last 10 minutes. At the end of a 200 minute testing session I might have a tally that looks like this.

Setup

IIII IIII

Coverage

IIII

Investigate

IIII II

Now with this simple memo I can quickly demonstrate the principle to my colleagues, clients and superiors. "This is a snapshot of my average testing session. This is how my time is distributed in general" I explain "You might see that I don't gain that much coverage because I tend to spend quite a bunch of focus on the other two areas. So it imposes a question on us. What could we do to regain our focus? What could we do to focus more on the coverage?" This tally and the accompanying question are priceless tools in scrum retrospects for example.

In setup we could come up with things like testability features and improve on our nightly build deployment automation. In investigation we could ask the development to improve on the crash dumps and logging mechanism of the software to make reporting bugs and hunting root causes faster and easier.

In conclusion, focus fuels results. If you want better outcomes, learn to lead your focus.

Chapter 10
Mindset Mistake #7:

Testing Makes Sure that the Software Works

The assignment was simple. This is the release candidate! Just test it and make sure that everything works and we can release it tomorrow by noon.

I still see a lot of testing assignments like the one above. There is an underlying assumption that testing can and must make sure that the software works; to assure colleagues and clients about this. But we cannot escape the truth. Testing is always a game of chance.

Let me explain it with a story…

Testing and the Creeping Death.

She had just taken her daughter to ballet practice. Now she had an hour to herself for her weekly run around the park while the little one danced. Her new running shoes felt great as she sprinted up the first hill. By the third hill she started to think something was amiss. Her feet felt heavy, breathing took extra effort and by the time the nausea hit her it was already too late. Darkness surrounded her senses as she collapsed at the top of the last hill.

The chest pain had first struck her at the swimming hall. That small sting in her upper abdomen must have been cramp or something. Maybe too much coffee in the morning? Increase the pace until the pain passes - that's what they had taught in school. Except that it did not. She had to stop and take a breath.

Some time passed and even climbing the staircase to the office had become hard. Eventually, that small sting came before she reached the second floor. She had to start taking the lift upstairs. In the end, there was a fine line between life and death. A matter of minutes passed, and a random act of kindness by a passer by. The stranger knew CPR and in addition to that was willing to do it while calling the emergency services. It took a full 20 minutes for the ambulance to arrive, but it did, just in time because the stranger was getting tired.

She woke up two days later in the intensive care unit of the local hospital and her first thought was for her daughter. Luckily a neighbour had taken the daughter home when she hadn't come back from the quick run around the park. It was an acute heart attack that had taken her by surprise. I held my breath while she told me the whole story. Life is a game of chance and the mind, it seems, is quite skilled in blocking out unpleasant facts.

"So was it a surprise for you?" I finally broke the silence after her story "No. All the symptoms were there" she told me. "Probably had been there for years, but I didn't mind. I had even fainted once before, but felt like everything was just fine. Until it wasn't. A traditional case of optimism bias" she concluded.

In the Second World War, the Germans were bombing London. The British command was afraid that the number of casualties during the first week might be as high as 250,000. As the bombings started, the media predicted that millions of Londoners would flee their homes and cause the British war industry to halt completely, handing ultimate victory to Hitler. The outcome was not as grim. There were 46,000 casualties, but amidst the ruins, the crazy Brits kept their calm and did not hesitate to carry on with their daily routines.

A Canadian psychiatrist J.T. MacCurdy explained the phenomenon by dividing the people into three different groups. The least meaningful, and the smallest group, as far as the explanation was concerned, were those who died in the bombings. The second group were the traumatised people, whom the bombs had wounded or who lost someone close to them. But they too were a small number compared to the entire population. The largest group by far were the third group of Londoners. The people, who heard the sirens, saw the bombers and could witness the explosions from afar, but were left physically unharmed.

MacCurdy noticed that being close to the crisis and feeling the tension related to it gave the largest group a false sense of invulnerability. The same phenomenon always seems to repeat when crises emerge. It increases the morale of the victims to unusual proportions. Illusions of invulnerability are beneficial to people who live among the terrors of war. They even bring people together to stand united in the face of terrorism. The human mind is incredible, but at the same time, so flawed.

The same mechanics, however, produces something called optimism bias. An unrealistic belief that we will avoid all harm tomorrow too. Every close call we have enforces the illusion of invulnerability. It happens in driving and sports as well as in software projects.

But now let me ask you the same question my friend asked me back then after she had recovered from the heart attack. What's in common with a creeping cardiovascular disease or Alzheimer's? Or the end of a marriage? How about cancer, alcoholism, bankruptcy or a software project that is about to crash and burn.

> "Not one of the things mentioned are within our control. Life is a game of chance."

My friend taught me that because life is a game of chance, we must hack the odds in our favour, because the tide might still turn against us. We must observe this truth every day. She has totally changed her lifestyle after the incident. Her new mindset is reflected in every action and decision she takes from diet to exercise to work. That is the way she hacks her odds. In addition to that she meditates and monitors herself constantly to spot signs of a possible attack early enough, just in case a second one comes. Now she knows the signs by heart.

> "The most important thing is to bypass the small, fearful voice inside the mind which assures us that everything is still just fine."

But now comes the testing side of the story. Testing is a constant effort to dispel assumptions and excuses. It is to find information about the software we develop. Once we see the truth more clearly, testing becomes a tool to tweak the odds in our favour, so that the project doesn't have to suffer a stroke just yet. Every bug we find is one obstacle less that needs to be found later in the game. One less reason for a customer to leave. One less iceberg in the sea of possibilities.

"But how then can we ever make decisions is such a setting?!" the manager might ask "We have to be sure before moving forward!" Yes! That might be true, and at the same time we must admit that this is more a matter of leadership than anything else. A former Navy SEAL commander Jocko Willink described the dilemma perfectly in his outstanding book "Extreme Ownership".

Navy SEALs and lethal assumptions

Imagine that you're a SEAL team leader with a difficult situation on your hands. The insurgents have taken the local police chief's nephew hostage and are holding him to ransom. YOU must get the boy out unharmed with your team.

Everything has been planned out meticulously. The team is ready to move on your command. But just at the last moment new intel arrives. There are IED's buried in the ground. Improvised explosives! And a machine gun in the house.

So as the team leader, What do you do?

The first impulse is natural. It might be not to go in, because it is not worth the risk. Maybe your impulse would be to abort the mission or to pause and re-plan. But then comes the hard question that NAVY Seals have a habit of asking:

> On which assignment can you be certain that there
> are no explosives buried in the ground or machine
> guns in the house?

Of course the answer is obvious. None. There can be no such mission where we can really be certain that there are no deadly explosives hidden somewhere. In fact this kind of assumption will be extremely lethal. As a software professional, this flags just one question in my mind. Demanding that the testing makes sure that software works is simply enforcing these lethal assumptions. Testing is a game of chance, so is the leadership of every project and so is life.

Instead of demanding certainty, help your management prepare for the what-if's just like the SEALs do! That is the role of a true testing guru. So, the next time you have launches and go-lives ahead. Plan like a SEAL. Gather intel. Don't make any assumptions. Prepare for the what-ifs. Hack the odds. Test.

> "No amount of experimentation can ever prove me right; a
> single experiment can prove me wrong."
> -Albert Einstein

No amount of testing can tell us that the software works, but at the same time even one test can prove that our software doesn't work. Stop testing now and the next test might reveal the hairiest showstopper ever. We have no way to know, so we have to play the game by the probabilities. Our job as testers is not to make sure that the software works. Our job as testers is to help the team build a Vegas-like setting where the house always wins.

Chapter 11
Mindset Mistake #8:

We Need a Spec to Spot a Bug

Last night we were sitting at the table eating dinner. On Sundays like this, we often dim the room and light a few candles. The candle light feels somehow enchanting as it flickers in the subtle movements of the air. As we ate, my son asked me if he could touch the flame.

"Of course you can." I replied "How do you think it will feel if you touch it?"

You don't need to be a rocket scientist to guess it will burn your finger. The same rules apply to licking a doorknob on a freezing winter day for example. The tongue is sure to stick there for a long time.

And it's the same with riding bikes too. Can you explain to me how you ride a bike? Yes, you have the pedals that you need to keep rotating. Yes, you need to keep the bike moving to be able to balance. Yes, there are the brakes and so on. But what would happen if you gave these instructions to a farmer in Nepal, who has never even seen a bike? Would he be able to ride it straight away? Maybe not. The thing here is that one needs to see and feel the bike. The process of trial and error is critical to eventually getting the idea of riding a bike.

The art of software development is full of knowledge that we stubbornly try to explain in different kinds of documentation, like the spec. But it will never suffice. Muscle memory, common sense or tacit knowledge doesn't work that way no matter how cerebral the activity may seem.

But what does this have to do with testing, you might ask?

The Lossy Method of Specification.

We played a game called Pictionary when I was younger. We would work in pairs, and one of us would take a picture card and try to describe or draw what was on it while the other one had to guess what it was. The outcomes were hilarious. Transferring even the most simple ideas with just words or a drawing is hard. The same game continues in our professional lives. We have a combination of requirement specs, drawings, functional and non-functional requirements from the customer. And then there are the business requirements that we need to translate into technical ones.

The problem that we will always have is that when the customer is different from the person doing the product development we have an air gap. The gap exists between the customer's mind and the developer's mind. And air gaps are always lossy! Traditionally we create specifications in order to freeze what the customers need, so that the developer doesn't have to try to hit a moving target. The challenge is to reduce the losses in the gap and ensure that the developer can accurately recreate what is inside the customer's head. As the complexity grows, the potential for error-creep increases.

Some time ago I got involved in a competition as an advisor. Some friends of mine developed solutions that would reduce the pressure on the Accident & Emergency departments in the UK's National Health Service. The team could come up with any ideas they wanted, but the competition requirements meant that they had to fill in an online entry form where they described the functionality of the product, the business plan, the financials and so on.

Each field was limited to 500 words. It took several weeks for the guys to put the application together. By far, the most significant challenge for them was to get the concept of the idea across in sufficient detail within the word count. Finally, the team had it, and they even recruited some support from within the industry. The guys had addressed a real-life problem in an innovative new way. But of course, they lost. Feedback was blunt. The judges didn't understand the proposal. To me, it seemed that it was merely an adult version of the game we played as kids. The point of the actual competition got lost in translation.

The specification is merely someone's speculation of how the product should work. In addition to that, it tries to reduce an infinite amount of mind-residing information to words on paper. Then, much later, the developer must try to expand that data once more to create a functioning product.

The only thing we can do is to accept the fact that not all knowledge can be written down on a piece of paper. The world is teeming with obvious causes and effects. We really do not need specifications to know what to expect. And that is why I say you don't need a spec to know if a candle burns and you cannot document how to ride a bike.

Testing is a piece of the development puzzle for a reason. To me, it is not to verify if the product matches the specification because then we only enforce the speculation and we never meet the original expectations of those who pay our bills. To me, testing exists to close those air gaps and to deal with the natural loss of information.

> "We do testing to build a broader band in a lossy channel of communication."

But how then, do you know when you've found a bug? If there is no all-encompassing specification that you can rely upon, then it must be some kind of intuition. How do you explain that hunch to others? It's not always straightforward to explain intuition in a professional way. I learned it the hard way with the vibrating dildo-phone in the earlier chapter Mindset Mistake #1, remember?

In that project everything worked perfectly and according to the spec but at the same time everything blew up on our face. The project got terminated along with our jobs. So how then, do we judge that a bug is a bug if we don't have a specification to hand? Or if we have a bug, how should we judge if it's worth the effort to fix it?

Is it Worth the Effort to Fix a Bug?

The attempts I've seen to classify bugs have focused on severity, impact, priority, risk, and reproducibility to name a few. No one keeps up with all criteria. In big projects, I've even seen them arrange big error meetings, and the organisation chart portrays a title called an "error manager". I've found that complexity is an enemy of execution. That is why I always aim at simple things first. In classifying bugs it has proven to be a binary decision. Either-or.

There are bugs that we need to fix and then bugs that we don't. But is there a sensible rule for making that kind of decision? Since gut feelings are not enough, we need something more concrete as the basis for our decision. Every business has a brand, a story, values, and a mind-scape of their own in addition to their product, of course. When all of these things match those of the audience, then the market tends to grow.

Consistency Builds Trust.

It's not the severity or the immediate impact of a bug that bugs me the most. Those are obvious criteria. What I look at first are the second order consequences of each bug. Every bug from the simple annoying one to the biggest showstoppers can all threaten the root cause of why we do business in the first place. In that sense every bug is created equal and to me those are the ones to look at most closely first.

A business usually becomes a success story only after our thinking, communication, and what we deliver are all aligned. That is why I've found that there is a single question that can give us clarity on each bug we analyse.

Does this bug threaten the things that we stand for?

This question is crucial, not only in reporting the bugs that we deem worthy, but in planning our future testing efforts too. We should not waste our time and money in testing things that we don't care about. Only after we understand the simple approach, should we dwell longer on the question.

How do you judge if a bug is a bug? The answer has everything to do with 5 principles of building awesome software.

The Half-life of Awesome

I still remember hearing the incredible sound of a dial-up modem connecting to the internet. It might be that I even got a little bit aroused by it. The whole world was literally at our fingertips. Being the teenage boys that we were, we immediately found an excellent application for it. It was boobs of course. But it doesn't take long for anything new and hot to become the new norm. These days I get frustrated when my phone drops its internet connection even for a second no matter the application. It's called hedonic adaptation. We human beings are neophiliacs to the core.

> "What is exceptional today, is the expectation of tomorrow."

It doesn't matter if we have invented something that creates a sense of awe. The expectations of our customers will soon rise up to the next level.

> "Awesome has a half-life, and it grows shorter by the day."

Knowing this, it's actually really funny to occasionally come across a project that aims for a minimum viable product. People both crave the novelty factor and at the same time hate software that sucks. There is no arguing about that. Viability is usually the argument for doing fast product development with a low threshold of adoption. But in fact, a minimum viable product is something that can kill the interest to begin with. Once the first impression is created, it is hard to change it.

So today, a much smarter move is to substitute viability with lovability. The aim is to build something that a few can fall in love with. But that is not the whole story in overcoming the hedonic adaptation. After the awesome becomes the new norm, you basically have two options to keep on being successful tomorrow.

> You can keep on inventing something new and awesome all the time, or,

> You can make sure that you consistently and reliably deliver what you promised.

Either way, you need to meet the expectations of your customers for a little longer to have a shot at break even or a viral success story of a scale up business. Let me give you an example.

It has been amusing to see how Instagram copies every single new idea that Snapchat introduces. These features then drip into Facebook and their Messenger app too. Now it will be interesting to see if LinkedIn updates the 24-hour stories into their feed.

If we are always the first ones to introduce new ideas, someone will soon copy the good ones and discard the bad. At the same time the awe we managed to produce becomes the new norm and we run out of the wow-juice fast. It's a hard race to win, so it all boils down to this set of questions.

> Can you consistently and reliably deliver what you set out to do?

Can you take out all the annoying little things that undermine the predictability of your product?

Consistently delivering on your core promises is key to succeeding long term. In software development terms you could say that anything which breaks the consistency between the expectations and your product is a problem that needs to be fixed. But as soon as we admit this, testers face a series of hard daily decisions. Here are a few examples.

Is it more important to have a product that is consistent with the requirements? OR with the ultimate purpose intended?

Is it more important to have a product that is consistent with the legal contracts OR with the image our company portrays in all of its communication?

Is it more important to have a product that is consistent with the vision of the few guarding the roadmap OR with habits and expectations of the audience?

The list could go on and on. The point is that we have to be able to deal with several shades of grey internally and at the same time, we have to be able to communicate clearly and decisively externally.

To make this paradigm easier for myself, I've developed a simple acronym. I call it HIPPE. Yep, there is no I in the word, but you pronounce it pretty much the same. The following five points are a set of consistency principles that I use in judging if my discovery is a bug and in explaining my intuition to others.

Principle #1: History

Something strange happened the moment I drove my new Ford Batmobile from the parking lot of my local car dealer. My son insisted we call the new car the Batmobile due to its dark grey colour. When I pulled the up to the first set of traffic lights, there it was in front of me. Another Batmobile, just like mine.

Only two blocks down the road I saw the second one in a different colour, then a third. Everybody had just found out how excellent this new Ford Focus is, I chuckled to myself, already guessing the malfunction of my mind. The human mind is a pattern recognition machine. In fact, it is such a sophisticated machine for patterns, that it craves familiarity.

Try crossing your fingers in reverse order. Doesn't it feel strange? For most of us, there is a pattern in crossing our fingers and the other ways just feels wrong. Because the human mind subconsciously wants certainty and a sense of control. Significant changes can cause unease and even resistance. This is why big deliberate changes in your software can be dangerous.

Similarly, failing at something that previously worked causes frustration and even anger. And this is the reason why regression bugs that cause the familiar things to fail can rapidly crumble the business you try to build.

Consistency between the product and its history is key #1.

Principle #2: Image

He was upset. Really upset. I could tell by the way he was acting and talking. Anger was boiling behind the face he portrayed in the meeting room.

"So what's wrong?" I asked him.

"Oh... nothing. I'm just super!" he faked a smiled back at me.

The atmosphere was tense, and it almost seemed like heavy rain clouds were hanging over him. Anybody could have seen that something was wrong. A week later I heard that his wife had filed for divorce. My instinct had not failed, but my friend was just not ready to talk about it. The inconsistency between his appearance and his actions made an impact on our software development team. Everyone noticed that something was wrong.

I've seen the same thing happen time and again with the software products. The company website portrays a polished image with fabulous promises about the product. At the same time, sales reps paint a picture of a better future too. Everything that happens prior to the decisions a customer makes builds a mental image in their heads. It creates expectations based on all that we show and tell our clients.

When the experience fails to meet the expectations that our public image portrays, it is a sure way to make our customers flee for the competitor's products.

Consistency between the product and the company image is key #2.

Principle #3: Product

Do you know what happens when you push Ctrl+F on Microsoft Word? Of course, you do. It's the "find" tool.

But do you know what happens when you push the same shortcut in Excel? Of course, you do. It's the "find" tool again.

But do you know what happens when you push the same shortcut in Outlook? You guessed it! It's not "find" there. It forwards the highlighted email message instead. But to make things more interesting, it does something else if there is no email highlighted.

If I was to develop a new office application, should I make sure that this specific keyboard shortcut works the same way as in every other office app out there? What would my ideal user expect?

Consistency between the product and itself, its siblings, and its rivals is key #3.

Principle #4: Purpose

For some reason I've always felt drawn to the work of Aristotle. I especially like his concept called teleology, which means that everything we perceive in the world has a purpose or goal behind it. No matter how simple the concepts might be. Like a fork, a room, a hand, a car, a road, a lamp or a phone. The purpose of a knife is to cut. Therefore sharpness is an essential feature of it. There is an ultimate purpose to your software product as well. If you were a product owner trying to build a business, the purpose might be different than if you were a user deploying this product for day-to-day use. But purpose there is. Always.

So with anything we perceive in the software product, we might want to ask. "Does this serve the purpose or not?" or "Does this thing threaten the ultimate purpose?"

Consistency between our product and its purpose is key #4.

Principle #5: Expectations

The four principles above demonstrate some of the expectations of our users or customers. They even shed some light on the expectations we might impose on ourselves as well. But could there be more? Are there other sources of expectation too?

Of course, we should be able to deliver what our legal documents, contracts or requirements expect. There might be standards like ISO that our industry should follow. Do we have a code of conduct or ethical guidelines to fulfil?

Most certainly we should not break the law or the EU GDPR legislation....Or kill anybody either. I'm sure you can think of even more sources of expectation.

Consistency between our product and external sources of expectations is key #5.

The Secret to Victory

It's always easy to deliver concepts, frameworks or checklists like H.I.P.P.E. But it's an entirely different thing to find a practical use for them. Marcus Aurelius once said that the secret to victory lies in the organisation of the non- obvious. But what, then, are the non-obvious things that are so elusive to many of us?

Usually, we work on lists of action points, phone calls, emails and tasks on the ticketing system. The daily flow of action and outcome hoards our attention and this is the obvious part. It's exactly the thing that we mostly see, the thing where most of our attention stays. So the very first thing we need to learn is to see what's in the background behind the noise of day-to-day work.

The non-obvious starts to emerge when we learn to stop and zoom our attention outwards. To take a step back and detach ourselves from the situation at hand. It's like being on a walk and suddenly noticing the birds singing in the distance. The birds probably were already there but your attention was somewhere else before you noticed them. At the moment of stopping and zooming we begin to see the structure behind the content. The structure is something that lingers everywhere just at the outer reaches of our perception.

> "There is always the wine and the bottle."

The non-obvious means the bottle where the wine resides. It is the context of the content. It means the structure which is the defining factor of all outcomes.

Within the trenches of daily action we tend to pay attention to the content, the obvious. We tend to re-create the same outcome we always get, because the structure of our work rarely changes. We end up filling the same container with familiar content. Yes, I know this might seem pointless at first, but let me give a few examples to put this idea into context. Look at the structure of your day in the calendar. Look at the structure of your route to work. Look at the structure of everyday conversations at the family dinner table. Look at the structure of a daily stand up meeting. Or the session of your exploratory testing. They all have easily recognisable patterns which are the non-obvious we want to focus on now. Remember, the secret to victory is in organisation of the non-obvious.

So, what if you stepped back right now for a while? Can you see the non-obvious here in your session of reading? How do you read? Or think your day. What's on your calendar next? Or what's for dinner today and how did you make that decision? Suddenly, when we learn to zoom out and see the non-obvious, new opportunities come within your reach. The change begins not by focusing on the content, it always begins by focusing on the context, by re-crafting the structure.

The Practical Application

H.I.P.P.E. is a structure too. Once we learn to see and shape these structures, we learn to transfer them to new environments and scale them in size as well. It's not only professional software testing, where we could use this concept. Consider these for example:

> Could you use this structure to explain your intuition about why a bug is a bug to others?
>
> Could you use this structure as a tool for story planning in your project?
>
> Could you organise out this week's testing efforts based on this structure too? How about your business strategy or the company brand?
>
> How about the product portfolio that your organisation has designed?

Now it's your turn. Where could you try this out today?

Chapter 12
Mindset Mistake #9:

Testers Break the Software

I was sitting on a train recently and since the bright morning sun prevented me from working, I decided to finish listening to a Hercule Poirot - audiobook I had started a week ago. It was Murder on the Orient Express which I found quite appropriate entertainment for a train trip.

Thankfully my trip was much less eventful, but once the book had finished, my attention was drawn to the other side of the aisle. Were any of my fellow passengers about to be turned into the next victim? I needed to check, just to be sure! Sitting around a four-seat table, was a group of business travellers. A guy was engaged in a loud telephone conference while occasionally talking with his colleagues next to him. After the call ended, he unplugged his 4G USB stick and started to pack.

"Don't tell me you just unplugged that stick?!" his colleague yelled. "Do you have any idea what might break? The VPN? email apps? What about our ERP?! You first need to turn off the connection from the menu, then remember to unplug the stick and only after that turn off the machine!"

As a tester, it was a curious transaction to observe. It occurred to me that the dude couldn't actually break the software by unplugging the USB stick. The software is already broken and the dude had just demonstrated how. Poirot never commits the murder or picks up a gun for that matter (except in the Orient Express -movie). The murder has already taken place and Poirot is the one who solves the mystery and then demonstrates how it was done.

It's the same with software testing too. The tester is the one who has been called upon to investigate the mysteries. The software is delivered to the examiner's desk as it is. Bugs don't miraculously appear in the software, instead they are already hiding inside the software at the start of testing. All mysteries await their investigator, someone to tear away the veil of assumptions and expectations.

> "The Tester's job is not to break the software, just the illusion of it."
>
> -James Bach

"Duh! That's obvious. How basic can you be seminar boy?!' a workshop attendee once asked me after I had explained what I mean by this specific mindset mistake. The question really was valid and it made me think. The idea is extremely basic, and at the same time it carries some implications with it too. Before dismissing the notion so willingly, I'd suggest a moment to dig deeper.

Saying that a testers' job is to break the software carries at least two kinds of implications.

#1 Psychology of Testing.

I believe that anything can be broken with enough force. If you've ever watched the Youtube video series titled "Hydraulic press" or "Does it blend," you'll know what I mean. I think that the same thing applies to software too. Every piece of software can be broken with enough effort, so the more important question is this. Is it truly purposeful to aim at doing that? To me it rarely is. As a professional, saying that my job is to break the software, easily sets my mindset on the wrong path. My job is not to focus on the force needed to break the software. Instead I must meet the needs of the business that I serve. To focus my psychology in testing, a more important question could be, for example, how much effort should we invest considering things like budget, risks or time?

The mindset of doing testing directly contributes to the second thing on my mind.

#2 Reputation of a Tester.

Saying that testers break the software is a public relations problem. Think about developers, managers, clients and executives. What if all the people we serve, harbour even a subconscious thought that testers only break their beloved things? How would that impact the dynamics of teamwork, the communication and the influence we testers have on others? I believe that the impact is mostly negative. Who on earth would want the things they build to be broken by somebody? Yes. It is true that anybody with intelligence can reason their way to a conclusion that breaking things actually helps in building bigger, better and shinier products, but at the same time the subconscious message is just the opposite. That is why we are exploring the concept of Storytools here. Do you still remember the triune brain that we discussed in the first chapter - Evolution of the Brain?

All of the communication created by our neocortex, the newest part of the brain, is deciphered by the deeper and older parts of the receivers brain. The parts that are responsible for things like intuition, emotions and fight or flight reflexes. From my inbox, to yours. Knowing this, I'd be very careful in using words like "break" in the context of testing. All of our reputation and influence as testing professionals is subject to the principles of the brain. So instead of thinking or saying that testers break the software, I've conditioned myself to rephrase it.

We do the work of Monsieur Poirot. We never break the software, we only show what it already does. Our job is to solve the mystery.

Chapter 13
Mindset Mistake #10:

Testing has No ROI

The explosion happened just 37 seconds after launch. The Cluster space craft provided us with one of the most expensive firework displays in the history of mankind, totalling a staggering $370 million. Cluster was a constellation of four European Space Agency spacecraft which were launched on the maiden flight of the Ariane 5 rocket on Tuesday, 4 June 1996. The launch failed due to errors in the software design. One of the main culprits being a simple integer overflow. The rocket veered off course just seconds after launch and self-destructed by way of the automatic flight termination system.

It turns out that the costly outcome was not the result of a showstopper bug. It was a result of incorrectly handling a trivial error. The software module responsible for the mistake was an inertial reference platform used in spacecraft to monitor acceleration, rotation and magnetic fields. The same software system was successfully developed and deployed in all the previous spacecrafts too, so it was obviously easy to assume the best case scenario. The only difference was that this new spacecraft could reach much higher horizontal acceleration than any of its predecessors. Pre-flight tests had never been performed on the inertial platform in the flight conditions of this specific craft and the trivial bug remained undiscovered. The integer overflow resulted from disabled assertions in the software. This caused the inertial platform computer and its backup to crash and emit corrupted diagnostic data. The autopilot did what it could with the data and so the blue touch paper was lit for the most famous fireworks display in history. The automatic self-destruction mechanism built for safety reasons worked flawlessly.

When studying software related incidents like this, it becomes evident that the root causes usually aren't the significant errors inside the system. It is far more likely that they are errors in the way our human habits handle these trivial errors. In situations like this one, testing never seemed important, until it was too late.

So what do you think that the return on the additional investment in testing would have been in this case? It is easy to be wise in hindsight, but "astronomical" would probably be the word to use in this case.

The ROI of testing is one of my favourite questions. Of course it's only natural, since part of my job for the past 12 years has been to sell testing services to people who didn't even know they needed them. In selling new ideas I've discovered that there are four things that beat common sense in decision making.

The Nobel prize laureate James M. Buchanan describes four secret motivations of individuals as a side note in his public choice theory relating to economics and politics. Common sense seems to be beaten by tradition, money, pride and power way too often in decisions of politicians, leaders and managers. If we step on someone's toes by violating their sense of heritage, sense of self or the position they think they hold, we're certainly going to trump common sense too. And then there is the money, an instrument of power like no other.

Most of these four secret motivations are matters of the limbic system and the lizard brain after all. Understanding this is crucial to planting your ideas into any organisation. Common sense often has nothing to do with how efficiently your idea is adopted, be it fixing a mindset mistake or anything else for that matter. So, if we as testing professionals wish to step up and change the organisations we serve, we must learn to address every secret motivation held within this model. And suddenly what we had dismissed earlier as the soft skills, seem like the real skills.

Every story hidden in this book is a way to hack the system to your benefit. Telling stories in order to demonstrate ideas doesn't usually threaten the tradition, pride or power of anybody. But what happens instead is that stories start growing as insights in others. And people are always more willing to believe their own insight than someone who comes telling them what to do.

So let's discuss Return on Investment (ROI) and money some more, because in testing it is a difficult topic. Testing, after all, is preemptive work and the true benefits are extremely hard to measure or calculate, because the alternative costs rarely emerge if testing was excellent.

Is There a ROI for Testing?

Now before proceeding any further, we need to get one thing about the ROI discussion straightened out. Have you ever taken music lessons? Can you still play? Are you any good at it? Could you make a living by playing? I can play the piano a bit. I took lessons while I was a kid. My dad took me every Wednesday after school. I also know how to skateboard. I learnt after seeing an awesome 80's movie called "Gleaming the Cube" starring the young Christian Slater. And I know how to drive a stick shift car too.

Yet, there is zero return on investment for me playing a piano, having a skateboard or getting a sports car. I have absolutely no idea what to do with those skills in order to make a living i.e. to build actual returns. At the same time the ROI of a piano is incredible for Elton John. He creates magic with his skill that nobody else can. Tony Hawk built a multi-billion dollar business on skateboards and Sebastien Loeb won the WRC rally championships 9 years in a row. That's what I call a return on investment!

Testing is no different. It is just a tool or a skill like any other. With piano, you need to be exceptionally skilled to reap the rewards and the same goes with skateboarding or motor racing. Luckily we don't need to be such superstars to deploy testing successfully. The point is, no matter what the tool is, there is always a return on the investment if you know what to do with it. If someone you know says they've tried testing before but it didn't quite work out, it doesn't mean that testing yields no benefit. It only means that they haven't yet learned a way to use testing to the team's advantage.

Testing works. There is no doubt about it. Testing has a ROI, but we first have to accept the preemptive nature of it.

The Mechanics of Returns

So now we are left with a question. What should we do to build returns? What are the different mechanisms that over time build returns on testing investments? I use a set of five principles or mechanisms about the ROI of testing that I'd like to see every testing professional learn to lay out for their peers, the people who have yet to be awakened.

Mechanism #1: Create the Reputation

I was a salesman of operator contracts and telephones a few decades ago. Back then most of the deals were done face to face. Comparing prices and products was hard back then, so, if anything, this was the dream situation for retailers. If you were lucky, you found a product review in a magazine or someone you knew had some first-hand experience with the product you were considering. Advertising and marketing also had a strong influence on decisions to purchase. My telephone-buying customers only came in to make up their minds about what to choose. Most of them had already visited a few different stores to compare prices and save a buck or two. But have you given a thought to how these decisions emerge today? Let's consider buying a new smartphone for example. What would I do as a potential customer?

- Look at a few reviews and unboxing videos on Youtube.

- Google how many stars it has received in reviews.

- Ask friends on Facebook and Twitter.

- Visit a few price comparison websites.

- Check the forums if there are any recurring warranty issues.

- Find out what the influencers of the domain say about this product.

- The list goes on and on.

Marketing is no longer traditional broadcasting about the product's awesomeness in the media. Modern marketing is about making sure that the product itself really is excellent. It's all about the influencers today! The products are supposed to offer outstanding experiences all the way from purchasing and unboxing, to the first minutes of usage all the way to the warranty handling process. Every single product today requires that their customers spread the sweet words of success. It will need someone to actually want to do the unboxing videos and share the photos on Instagram. Inferior products might have had a chance of succeeding a few years ago while the most visible ads and face to face sales encounters were able to influence the decision of a customer.

But today that kind of approach would be like playing the lottery. The only option is to invest in the quality of the actual product.

So the first mechanism of ROI in testing is simple:

Testing is a way to increases the odds of success. This is achieved by first improvements in quality that will eventually lead to the growth of your reputation, and revenue. If you can't explain it to your peers, no one will do it for you!

Mechanism #2: Handle the Exceptions

Do you have a lock on your front door? Do you keep it locked? I have one on mine and I do, but have you ever given a thought as to why it is there? It's not for the real burglars. If someone really wanted to break in, then they would do so, no matter what. There are crowbars, lock picks and other tools of the trade to either hack the system or use brute force to get in.

The lock is there to prevent the entry of regular uninvited people. Those who just try their luck to see if it has been left open. It is true that businesses focus more on their security with surveillance cameras, alarm systems, motion detectors and personal RFID keys. But do you know how secure that excellent new web service you are developing is? Is it like an unlocked bicycle, a regular home office or a well guarded Fort Knox of your most precious things? And if you know, can you elaborate the reasons for deciding if it is enough?

I'm still surprised about how many software projects are caught off guard with this question. Exactly the same thing happens when somebody asks if the software can handle the Black Friday traffic smoothly? Nobody seems to know. The responsibility lies in the grey zone of that mysterious person - "someone else."

Uninvited visitors and the traffic peaks are always an exception, of course. And the same goes for functional errors too. Testing is there to handle and prevent unwanted exceptions. Yes, this is Captain Obvious talking again, I know. But to really squeeze the juice out of this, I'll give you a tool which I learned from a business guru Keith Cunningham and his book "The Road Less Stupid".

There are three questions that a professional should always remember to ask when making decisions about investments.

1. What's the upside? In some businesses, being the most secure service provider out there and being able to prove it, is a leverage for marketing like no other. The same goes for being a super performer during the busiest business days of online marketplaces like Christmas or Black Friday. Some online stores even report doing 80% of their revenue in just 10 business days of the year.

> => If you want the upside, do testing!

2. What's the downside? Think about a marketing campaign gone viral on Facebook. Those moments are priceless and rare. The downside can be catastrophic if the website was down those crucial first hours of the rush. And the security! Now we have the GDPR regulations in Europe. Let the personal data of your client leak, and you might get fine for up to 4% of the company revenue. It would mean losing 400k€ on 10M€ revenue.

> => If you don't want to risk it, do testing!

3. Can we live with the downside? Now this third question is one that only a real pro remembers to ask. A secret part of the skill in creating ROI out of testing is knowing when not to test. Because there is always a risk of testing too much or testing the wrong things and that for sure will waste our precious time and money.

> => If you can live with the downside, don't test!

So if you are a tester, now would be a great time to do the people you work for a favour. Ask them about the locks or the Black Friday and see what happens. So the second mechanism of ROI in testing is simple:

Testing is a way to take care for the downside and boost the upside! Your job as a professional is to help peers understand this. If you can't explain it to your peers, no one will do it for you!

Mechanism #3: Do the Maths

Do you remember the story at the start of this chapter? The Cluster spacecraft and the $370 million fireworks? Stories like that are a way to describe the monetary value of an error. But to take the practice even further here is another one.

The U-2 was a spy plane, developed in the 1950s by Lockheed for spying on The Soviets during the cold war but it is still in service to this day. What is unique about the plane, is its light structure and the high altitude it can fly. It can climb to over 100,000 feet (~30,5 km). An altitude that high is rare even for more modern planes. Los Angeles airport learned this the hard way in April 30th, 2014. The flight control system was not designed to handle the altitudes that the U-2 reaches and their system malfunctioned.

A simple software bug caused the system to interpret extreme altitudes as really low ones. Just a simple overflow in handling long numbers. It forced air traffic control into a chain reaction of readjusting the flight routes of every single plane in southern California. The system could not handle the load, and all air traffic control in southern California was left paralysed for an hour. 50 flights were cancelled and 27 were rerouted to different airports and 455 other flights were delayed. Other airports in the area had to do the same.

I always get curious when reading about these kind of incidents. My first impulse is to try and calculate the costs of such events. Of course the calculation is only a play with numbers, but it creates some kind of a reference point to the reality. Even if the numbers are not entirely correct.

A little bit of Googling finds out that a flight from L.A. to New York could cost an airline $56,400. The expenses are mostly there whether they fly or cancel that flight. Then there is the loss of revenue that would increment the damage significantly. 50 such cancellations would easily cost the airlines $2,820,000. I wonder how many similar scenarios related to this one incident we could come up with if we tried? The total cost of this one incident could climb up to tens of millions.

These kind of hypothetical calculations help a lot in explaining how the ROI actually emerges if we did testing. With a bit of practice you could learn to perform this kind of calculations on a whiteboard in front of your customer. But the story does not end there. There is one more calculation we need to do. How much software testing could we have bought with that money?

Let's consider an expensive test consultant with a $200 hourly fee. How many days could that kind of a professional work with money like $2,820,000? (Answer: 1763 days)

Now to put things into perspective. Think about just how many similar bugs we could have caught with that kind of an investment? Testing is the preemptive craft of saving the business we serve. That is why we can never know how big the scenarios we successfully prevented. Two ways to demonstrate it are learning to create calculations based on a hypothesis of bugs we've already found. Or searching and memorising enough real world case descriptions along with their numbers to build perspective.

So the third mechanism of ROI in testing is simple:

Testing is a preemptive craft with no apparent returns beforehand. You as a testing professional need to know those numbers and learn to talk money. If you can't explain it to your peers, no one will do it for you!

Mechanism #4: Testing Saves Money

When was the last time you had a vaccine? I had one just before the flu season last year. Access to essential vaccines around the world gets easier by the day. Humanity has been victorious against smallpox saving an estimated 5 million lives annually through an efficient vaccination program. In addition to that, it seems like we might soon be victorious against polio too. According to an expenses-analysis made few years ago in the USA, every dollar invested in vaccination now reduces overall health care expenses by $2-$27.

But have you ever stopped to think what long term savings software testing might be able to achieve from in things like customer retention, legal issues with contracts and schedule, warranty returns or refunds and critical patches.

When I'm approached and asked to help with testing, it often happens during the final phases of the product development. Downstream on the timeline, some would say. Yes, you remember this from the chapter Mindset Mistake #2. In such situations, the development might have been rolling along for years, but now three weeks before a major new release, we suddenly come up with the idea of actually testing the product. That's pretty daring, I would say.

Just this morning I came across a paper entitled "The Economic Impacts of Inadequate Infrastructure for Software Testing." It was prepared for The National Institute of Standards & Tech in the U.S. in 2002. According to the research, the cost of discovering and fixing a bug increases rapidly when compared to finding the same problems at the requirement design stage.

> It would cost 90 times more if we found the bug in system testing phase.
>
> It would cost 440 times more if we found the bug just before delivering the software to the customer.
>
> It would cost 470–880 times more if the customer found that bug.

Of course, this is an old concept and rolling out hot fixes and patching bugs is now easier than ever before. For example, Apple rolled out three iOS updates in three weeks after releasing the iOS 11 in September 2017. On the other hand, consider the incredible amount of hassle related to car manufacturers like VW and Audi with their software updates in the CO_2 scandal. The multipliers are probably way higher for them.

It all depends on the industry. Just like a colleague of mine found out while he was building a house. Part way through the build, he changed his mind about something. He wanted the bathroom to have two showers instead of one, and he needed to rework the plumbing before tiling the floor. It had been a long week of construction work when the plumber finally arrived to install the showers and the washing machine. Before starting the job, the plumber had a brief discussion with my colleague. He wanted to know if there were pipes for floor heating in the bathroom. Of course, there were, that was one of the comforts of this design.

Before starting the work, the plumber decided to run a set of tests. He blew pressurised air through the pipes to see if everything was ok to proceed. A pillar of dust burst through the floor — the heater pipes had failed. Had the plumber simply got on with his job without first testing the previous work, we would have been looking at extensive water damage in a newly built house. My colleague would have had to renovate the bathroom and the adjacent room within a few months of moving in. In this case, they got away with only re-installing the floor pipes. Not a significant expense compared to what could have been.

Though we might never be able to accurately tell how big an impact this plumber had on the house building project, it seems apparent that he saved more money than he took. To me, that is enough.

Though we might never be able to accurately tell how big of an impact each polio vaccination has on humanity, it seems apparent that it saves more lives than it takes. To me, that is enough.

Though we might never be able to accurately tell how big of an impact early testing has on the software we develop, it seems apparent that is saves more than it takes. To me, that is enough.

So the fourth mechanism of ROI in testing is simple:

Testing is saving. The earlier you do it, the more it saves. Increasing returns is just a byproduct of testing. If you can't explain it to your peers, no one will do it for you!

Mechanism #5: Boost Productivity

Digging through old lines of code to fix a bug is like digging through a big box of old family photos. Remember? This is exactly what we discussed in the chapter Mindset Mistake #2. To save your time and mine, I'll just head on to the conclusion.

So the fifth mechanism of ROI in testing is simple:

Testing boosts productivity. The closer we are to the development, the faster the feedback. A fast feedback loop makes it easier and faster to fix bugs, prevent regression and promote rapid learning. An increase in productivity is a byproduct of testing. If you can't explain it to your peers, no one will do it for you!

Compound Interest Rates.

You can pay the price now or later. If you choose to pay later, then it will always come with interest. I could, for example, take my next vacation using my hard-earned savings, or I could do it with a quick swipe of a credit card and then keep on paying until next summer. Which way is sustainable?

Health has a price too. I could invest time and money to exercise and mostly have sweat and aching muscles as a reward. In the kitchen I'd make better decisions and even some sacrifices to stay fit. On the other hand, I could slack off now and pay later when the doctor advises me to change or die. Which way is more sustainable?

The five mechanisms described in the previous subchapters are just a part of the world which creates significant returns on testing investments. The returns are real and very achievable in skilled hands, just like with a piano, skateboard or a racing car. The biggest obstacle for seeing this, though, is the human tendency for impatience. We always seek the quick fixes and the shortcuts. We're on the constant lookout for the new tactic that would make things easy and fast. It's no wonder that the health and fitness industry is thriving. I know several people who have a closet full of miracle pills and an attic full of TV show devices they never use.

With the ROI of software testing, the thinking tends to follow a similar path. The discussion revolves around trying to figure out if a week or a month of testing pays off or not? It still seeks the quick fix or shortcut. That's a real dilemma I have to admit. There is no way to accurately measure things such as the direct correlation between money spent and the amount of incoming support tickets. Software testing and quality emerging in its wake is a long term game and the impact cannot be reliably observed in the short term.

In this situation I usually advise the management to focus on bugs found and the opinions of developers. On the other side of the table, I advise the testers to focus their effort on finding bugs and making sure that the developers will cry out if you were to leave!

But now let's play the long game for a few minutes. Have you heard about technical debt? Simply put, it's a concept that reflects the cost of reworking the mistakes that are caused by taking the easy way instead of the wise way. The concept is named a debt for a reason. Choosing the easy way will consistently cause a growing need to fix and rework the codebase later. The amount of work needed to recover eventually grows like a life form. It will accumulate interest just the same way a credit card debt does. The thing that is common to all interest is that compounds. Here is an example.

Johnny takes a $30,000 loan for renovating his home with an annual interest rate of 5% and a 10 year payment plan. In the end he is left with a total repayment of $38,000. Basically he paid $8,000 extra.

Tina, on the other hand, invests a $30,000 in an index fund with 5% interest for 10 years. In the end she is left with $49,000. So basically she just earned $19,000 without doing any kind of work.

In the end Tina is left with $27,000 more than Johnny. Increasing the debt is a surefire way to get poor and stay that way. Interest and the power of compounding either works for us or against us. And you know what? This is one of the underlying reasons why the rich seem get ever richer and the poor seem to get ever poorer. Lucky for us, that we understand the mechanism of interest compounding and have the freedom to choose for ourselves.

Now comes a question for you. What is the opposite of technical debt in your software project? For most the answer would revolve around investing time and money somewhere, so where is it for you? In my experience, most successful projects seem to over-invest in quality in advance, while most of the disasters are a result of using a credit card mentality instead.

To conclude, I have only one piece of advice which applies to software projects too.

If you desire success in important things like health or wealth, there are no shortcuts. You must learn to pay upfront.

Chapter 14
Mindset Mistake #11:

Automation is the Cure-All

Test automation is about making sure that things still work. It is about continuously monitoring that nothing we are working on has broken overnight. Automation gives us fast feedback and it never grows tired of re-running the same checks. There is just one thing you should not forget about automation. You will always get what you asked for, and this is why you need to be extra careful about what you order. How can you be sure you are asking for the right things? How can you even be sure that you are creating the right kind of features in your product in the first place?

"Well, I suppose I can't. It's kinda complicated."

True. Building software is always complicated. Automation gives you binary feedback. It either passes or it doesn't, and it does the same without error again and again. There will be no shades of grey. It is true that automation builds confidence regarding decision-making. But in the end, it only provides an assurance about the things we think we want, at the time we set the script in place.

Do you still want the same things tomorrow? Or next week? Or a year from now?

> "Well, I suppose I don't know. It's kinda complicated."

True. Building software is always complicated. Automation only sets a fixed point in time about the things you want at that specific moment. There will be no shades of grey.

Confidence, certainty, and assurance are great goals and automation will certainly deliver those. But how can you be certain that the certainty is warranted? How can you make sure it's not a false confidence?

> "Well, I suppose I can't be sure. It's kinda complicated."

True. Building software is always complicated. Once you place that order, you need to be extra careful about what you wished for. The automation will deliver exactly what you ordered. There will be no shades of grey.

In the world of automation, you will always get what you ask for, and that is why the burden of responsibility grows heavy on you.

So. Are you up for it?

If your answer is still "kinda yes" then let's move on. Automation is amazing at giving fast feedback and it never grows tired of re-running the same checks.

This notion is worth investigating further. Do you still remember when we talked about the paradox of quality assurance and blueberries? Testing is the sum total of two very different activities.

Checking was one of them. Checking is the repetitive work aimed at building confidence and producing evidence as a track record. Confidence however needs to be warranted. No one in their right mind would want false confidence to base their decisions on. So we need an opposing force, which is to destroy the false confidence that checking easily builds. We need something to dispel the illusions. We need hunting.

Hunting was the second activity. It is the part where we go out into the woods to put all of our experience and creativity as explorers into play to get a bucket full of those plump berries, it's about finding more bugs.

Checking is a factory-like process, while hunting is deeply creative work. The same methods of management or execution don't apply to them. So with an automation discussion, first and foremost, you need to return to asking the familiar question. What are the outcomes we desire from our testing? Evidence or bugs? Assurance or dispelling of illusions? Control or freedom? Production line or adventure? Metrics or creativity? Checking or hunting?

This decision is constantly in the making. For every testing assignment, for every time box, for every test plan and company wide strategy. If we want to do a good job with our quality, there is no escaping the question. The automation is not the cure-all for testing. It might work for the outcomes of checking, but so far I have never seen an AI that is capable of creative thinking or producing something out of nothing, an AI capable of creativity and hunting. In other words generating new ideas out of thin air, like humans do.

So basically this mindset mistake results from not understanding our berry-picking story. I've got to repeat the conclusion once more because I believe it is the most important takeaway of the entire book.

This mistake results from not understanding that testing is the sum total of two very different activities, namely checking and hunting.

Four Pitfalls of Test Automation

At the beginning of last year we made a bold assumption. Test automation can be sold as a productised service. This means that we could make a promise to our client that we would create the base of automation and automate a handful of acceptance tests in a tight two week project with a fixed price tag. Our clients were ecstatic and so were we. "It's going to be huge" we celebrated.

It turned out to be a disaster instead. We sold automation packages like crazy and proved our assumption totally wrong. In the end our customers were satisfied, but the amount of work we put in to achieve the results far exceeded what we got to invoice. The experiment cost us a total of 250,000€ in losses. Some learning money, I've got to admit.

From these experiences we digested four pitfalls of automation that most projects fall into when they attempt automation without a clear vision.

Pitfall #1: Falling in Love with a Project Mindset

I was in a meeting with the board of directors of a client. Their business domain is one of the more traditional ones as they have a factory producing metallic machine parts for their clients. The CIO was explaining how they had a team of three full time developers from a consultant firm doing digitisation projects. I got curious and asked how long these developers had been working on the projects? The CIO shared that the team actually started on their first project two years ago and were supposed to be done in six months. Then a need to continue the project arose and at the same time four more projects came in to work on. And now the three consultants who came in for a six month project had been in a loop of consequent projects for over two years.

The CEO was one of the silent kind and was listening quietly to our conversation when he suddenly interrupted. "Hey guys" he said, "to me it seems like this digitisation is not a project at all. To me it seems like this is our new way to live and breathe." There was no way to disagree. I had to sit in that meeting to finally understand what was going on with our testing team attempting to figure out the test automation puzzle worth 250,000€. To consider test automation (or digitisation) a project is like trying to hit a moving target in 100m with a handgun. If you've ever tried it, you know what I mean. Only Ethan Hunt or James Bond could do it with precision. The rest of us must rely on luck.

Automation is not a project. It's a new way to live and breathe.

Pitfall #2: Falling in Love with the Hardware Store

A picture rail is a smart device because you can hang paintings from it at any height and anywhere in the room with just a piece of string to support the weight of the painting. And the best thing is that you don't need to drill any holes into the wall, so moving and replacing art is a breeze. My picture rail sat gathering dust in a closet for three years. During that time, I even moved to a new apartment. That rail just didn't find its way to its intended place. It said on the instructions that I should install it on the wall close to the ceiling. Wow! Didn't think of that one! It turns out though, that I have a problem that is not unique. I just couldn't get started on the job. First I would need to go to the hardware store to buy tools. I would need a new ladder, some special screws and of course worker pants, which could hold all the other tools I thought I might need. When you stop to think about the problem a bit more closely, the solution is evident.

Finally, after years of procrastination, I got up on the kitchen stool and broke a little sweat by screwing the rail in by hand. It only took me 7 minutes, and I bet nobody would even notice the difference. Maybe it's not about the tools after all? Maybe it's just hard to get started, and the hardware store was my excuse.

Automation is like the hardware store and it easily becomes the excuse.

Pitfall #3: Falling in Love with the Hammer

I have a colleague. They call him the Doctor, and there is a reason for that. He has a track record of solving impossible test automation problems with speed and precision. The Doctor faces one question on a regular basis. What tools does he use or recommend?

I have the heart of an engineer, and maybe that is the reason why his answer always takes me by surprise.

> "It is true that you can drive in a screw with a hammer. But it would be easier to first find out what we are really trying to do here - and why."

There is always the one danger in professional work. Trying to solve problems by first defining the toolset is expensive and time-consuming. Running enthusiastically is great, but if you run in the wrong direction, you end up in the wrong place. Much the same way with testing tools, we all too easily end up addressing the wrong questions. So what is the Doctors answer to the question of what tool he uses?

Fall in love with the hammer and you will only ever see nails.

Pitfall #4: Falling in Love with the Price Tag

It had been a cold night and the morning frost was still covering the grass. The sun was rising above the horizon. I was sipping my morning coffee on my terrace and listening to the birds singing in the forest nearby. A distant buzzing noise penetrated the quiet Saturday morning. I recognised the sound since I had heard the noise many times before. It was the neighbour's Robomow taking care of the lawn. This time something wasn't right, though. Despite its best efforts to get free, the masterpiece of gardening technology was stuck in the roots of an apple tree. The neighbour had left for work, so I kindly loosened the robot and carried on with the coffee.

But what if that lawn represented our product. The automation kept covering it in peace. Everything was just fine until the unexpected happened. Automation requires human attention to break free from the apple tree.

A typical misconception is that automation can replace a human. This is the basis of a belief that automation will lead to cheaper testing. That there might somehow be an amazing ROI.

I bought my own Robomow just recently. I can tell you it took quite some time to set up the perimeter wire that keeps the robot in my garden. And to teach it the areas it should handle. And still, it routinely gets stuck on one steep slope and another set of young bushes at the back of my yard. I go out and free it every morning. The robot was not cheap of course and the cost grew the more time I spent getting it working. In addition, the robot needs regular maintenance. Luckily, I love playing around with tech, so it was a fun investment. And the lawn looks fantastic!

Now some months later it seems that the investment has finally started to save some time. Automation sets my hands free of the repetitive and boring stuff, to pursue higher goals. But it wasn't evident in the beginning. I'm not sure how many summers it will take for my household to break even with this investment, but I believe it will be close to 4 years. In case you plan to invest in automation in your project, I would urge you to remember this. When you plan automation, know your costs and design how you will break even. If you don't plan the ROI, no one will do it for you!

The price is never the cost. You pay the price today and the costs add up over time.

Automation Nibbles at our Job

Now, I've been to countless conferences and seen many talks about test automation. Almost all of the talks have a slide that says something like "Automation is not going to replace you". I say that's total nonsense. Compared to humans, automation already does a better, faster and more reliable job with anything from watering plants to trading stocks, reading legal documents, diagnosing medical conditions and flying an intercontinental flight.[9] The automation centred discussion in software testing remains the same as it was almost ten years ago. We discuss how there are "automated testers" and there are "manual testers" For some reason it feels natural for us software people. But what if we were discussing automated doctors and economists or manual scientists? Sounds ridiculous, doesn't it? Would you get on an aeroplane with only a manual pilot? I wouldn't for sure. We could argue the ethics, benefits and applications of automation forever. We could wrestle with the notion of titles and naming conventions in our profession, but one thing always remains. Automation is an increasing part of our everyday life. It nibbles away at our field of work. Day in and day out, the advance of automation keeps on taking the obvious, recurring and complex tasks from our hands. That is what a thermostat already does for us. And what flight searching portals do faster than any human could. Nobody makes any fuss about the automation already in place there. Yet still we insist on having a discussion of manual vs. automated testing. It's like we are stuck in a loop at the edge of tomorrow.

Our professional advantage comes from our skill to learn and utilise all the automation that is already at our disposal. The only question is, will we actually do it? Forget the biased arguments and start thinking about this. What is it that you can do, that is really hard for a computer or an AI to execute? Then start drilling. And drill deep.

Automation is an Extension of Us

The question was simple, yet so complex. Steve Jobs sat in the interview as silence fell for a brief moment.

---

[9] Every rule needs its exception. Its funny how for some reason machine brewed coffee never tastes as good as homemade. Even though the water temperature, the bean grind and the pressure are all optimal with no variation compared to manually brewing. What is the human factor that makes the difference?

"What is that personal computer?" the interviewer
had just asked and the answer blew me away,

"A computer is the bicycle for the mind" Steve said,
and let the silence fall once more.

As a 12 years old, Steve read an article in Scientific American that he still clearly recalled. It was a study of the efficiency of locomotion for different animals. The Condor won, since flying consumes the fewest calories for Condors. Humans were somewhere down the list with their inefficient energy consumption. But as the scientists tested the boundaries further, they discovered that humans win the race every time when they use an efficiently designed bicycle.

Human beings are a species evolved to design tools that up their game. The computer is the bicycle for the mind. That is what automation is.

Chapter 15

Yours is the Next Story to Tell

Wow. You're exceptional. We meet here after working through 11 mindset mistakes of software testing. It's not an achievement that can be taken lightly. Did you know that the attention span of the average human is enough to read a computer screen worth of text and not much more. Some studies even propose the attention span is shorter than that of a goldfish, less than 7 seconds to be precise[10]. So if you've come this far it means that you're above average. I'm impressed!

Now you might think that there must be more mindset mistakes out there. Like something to do with metrics for example. And you're right, there are a lot. And now that you've got the drill it's your turn to start creating. What is

---

[10] Yes! The science behind this might be a bit wobbly, but the idea is fun to contemplate anyway!

the one idea about metrics that you want to make stick? Write it down in your journal and preferably iterate it towards a Twitter friendly format with a maximum of 280 characters, or 140 if you're old school and hardcore!

The next thing you will need is a supporting story or a parable to make that point. Dig in to your memories and write down as many ideas about incidents from your life as you can. They might revolve around competitions you've attended, games you've played with friends or asking your mom to measure how tall you were every week at the age of six when you wanted so badly to be bigger. They can be funny, they can be insightful and they can be touching incidents. It doesn't matter, as long as they emotionally connect YOU in some way. And remember. It's easier to tell the truth, because that's what you remember and that's what engages you the most. Then comes the hard part. You need to tell that story to someone. Either you tell it as a bedtime story to your kids and see how it feels. Or you might tell that story to your diary in writing. It doesn't matter how you do it, as long as you do it. The final part is to tie the story to the idea you wanted to make stick. You might even start by asking 'So what can we learn from this story?'

Let me share one more of mine as an example. This one is about metrics.

Metrics and the Mystery of Bricked Windows

For reasons unknown to me, part of the windows were bricked shut on every street. It was spooky, almost as if a dead body had been buried inside the wall. And it seemed like it had been a common hobby for people at some point of history.

I was on a vacation trip to the city of Bath, some 200 km west of London. It was a beautiful countryside drive after an awesome series of testing workshops at the London Tester Gathering. The strange windows immediately caught my attention. I had seen similar windows before in France but had just dismissed the notion back then. It was on that trip to Bath when the mystery of these spooky looking windows was resolved.

As it turns out, the trend was set in motion in England, France, Ireland and Scotland when King William III decided to impose a new tax law in 1696. The law was designed to levy taxes relative to the prosperity of the taxpayer. It was assumed that the prosperity could reliably be measured by the size of the homes people lived in. Rich people lived in bigger homes and could therefore pay more tax. The easiest way to measure prosperity of course was to count how many windows each one had. So the window tax was invented.

It doesn't take genius to invent ways to pay less tax in this setting. People quickly learned to brick their windows shut. Less windows meant less tax. And then of course there were the few who wanted to show off by building even more windows in to their homes as well.

But why would I tell you this? What can we learn from this story?

For one, It makes no difference what kind of metrics we decide to use. People have always been good at playing games. It's not a question of how reliable your metrics are.

The real question is: Which games are already played with them?

Chapter 16

The Three Powers of Leadership

#1: The Power of Daring

I like to play with ideas. Will you join me for a small thought experiment? I took this one from Seth Godin, one of my intellectual idols.

Let's assume you owned a conference facility. What would you do with it? What kind of an event would you organise? Which one thing would you choose that would get you truly sparked up in the morning, every morning?

I'm not sure if you stopped reading to think about it, but I had to stop writing for a moment. For me it would be something creative, like a TEDx event or a storytelling workshop. Now, here's the big idea. You could actually own that conference facility one day at a time. So why don't you already?

Time, boss, money, organisation, process, strategy, energy and timing are some of the most common reasons. These are the easy excuses for placing the blame elsewhere and not doing something truly inspiring. But I'd say we got it all wrong. The reasons mentioned are only a list of resources. What we lack in execution is resourcefulness. Tapping into the potential of personal resourcefulness has just one precondition. It's the skill to place all of the blame inside oneself. That is the part of taking ownership for everything we face.

The biggest obstacle to ownership is not intellectual, it is emotional. Most of life's big things are.

The reason I'm willing to propose that most of our problems are emotional by nature, is simple. Intellectual problems are solved by a matter of reasoning and finding tactics and strategies. And the world is full of those. You can prove this by simply opening Google and trying to find a how-to for your issue. For most problems, the answers are plentiful and only rarely do we have problems that someone else hasn't already solved. The only obstacle for us is that we don't follow the advice we find. We don't stick with the plan long enough for the results to come.

If our problems were only of an intellectual nature, all new year's resolutions would be kept, most diets would never fail, everybody would stick to their gym plan and most businesses would flourish too. Oh, and my all time favourite. Marriages would always succeed.

But that's not how the world really works. Success is never about the tactics available or the intellect we deploy. We might be really good at advising our friends in what to do with their lives or diets or anything else for that matter, but at the same time it is really hard to act on our advice for our own benefit. Hence, I repeat myself. The biggest obstacle to every breakthrough in our lives is emotional, not intellectual.

Once we choose to own all of our circumstances, in other words we decide that we are responsible for all the things in our experience, the resourcefulness starts flowing thick and fast. So I invite you to consider this. What if you could be the champion of a cause? Which cause would it be? For Columbus it was about finding the sea route to India and according to a popular story, he started with just an egg.

The Egg of Columbus

> "Here is an egg" Columbus began
>
> "Now show me how to make it stand on its end on this table" He was facing potential sponsors for his future voyages and could only rely on his skill to plant the seeds of ideas into the minds of the audience.

At the meeting, everyone took their turn to try the feat. Nobody succeeded. The egg always fell to its side. Finally Columbus stepped forward with the big reveal. He tapped the tip of the egg hard on the surface breaking it, and behold! The egg stood on its end.

The trick is easy to replicate once you know how it's done, of course. And that was his whole point. When one finds a new route, it is easy for everyone else to follow.

The Copernicus of Today.

Nicolaus Copernicus was the first to present the indisputable proof of the heliocentric Solar System. He dared to claim that the Earth orbits the Sun! I can't help but wonder how he felt at the time. The church opposed him since The Bible said that the Earth was the centre of the Universe.

Let's build a bonfire and burn the heretic!

A hundred years later a fellow called Galileo Galilei brought up the heliocentric theory again. The church still did not like it, but little by little the evidence started to overtake their beliefs. Now take a look at the school books of today. We have come a long way!

It always takes time for such a shift in thinking to take place. Luckily for us, we don't need to wait for hundreds of years for such miracles anymore. Getting exposure for your ideas is easier than ever. Distributing your new thought or concept has never been faster. And it is likely that no one wants to burn you at a stake for it either. At least, not literally!

Yet, it is always easy and feels safe to follow someone else. To keep your head down in the shadow. To hope that the pathfinders risk everything in order to show others the way to follow. It feels easy and safe to wait for someone else to demonstrate how the trick is done. Laying low might have been the safest option centuries ago, lest you wanted to be deemed a witch. But today I'm willing to propose that the safety zone has moved.

Being a good husband or wife does not protect us from a divorce. Being a good employee does not protect us from being laid off. It feels unfair, I know, but we need to face the truth of it. Being good is not enough anymore. We need to play our game on levels way higher than before. We need courage to stand out. We need to become outstanding because that is where the safety zone of today is.

To me, this is the core of true leadership. It was never about organisation charts or the processes we follow. It's not about the tools we deploy or the titles we hold on our Linkedin profile. An outstanding professional, takes ownership and is willing to lead. That kind of professional goes where there are no trails to trample and leaves a path for others to follow. A true professional takes one egg at a time and shows everyone. The chances are, that if you've come this far with me, you are the Copernicus of today.

So if there was a cause that you could be the champion of, which cause would it be? How would you wield the Storytools in order to spark a change? Would you unite a group of customers, co-workers, hobbyists or friends by daring to go first and following it up with the two most simple words of leadership?

Follow me.

As Helen Keller once said.

"Life is a daring adventure or nothing at all"

#2: The Power of Patience

Hah. That was quite a pep talk there. Now that we're all psyched up, I've got to break in with the truth. Change and leadership are not that easy, but you probably already knew that by experience. People around us often seem like idiots, they never listen and nobody really changes. Or at least so it seems. Well, that's the reason this book was created in the first place. Change is a matter of our skill in leading the culture. And culture is a thing that has fascinated me for a long, long time. Have you ever given a thought to the word itself? Culture by its origins means to cultivate plants or even bacteria. In agriculture, for example, it means improving the soil and the land to bring better crops at the time of harvest. In growing chili peppers I've noticed that there is virtually nothing I can do to the plant itself to get a better crop. The plant does what the plant wants to. And it's the same with the culture inside our teams and organisations. In creative work like the software industry, people have a tendency to revert back to their old familiar habits.

The only way to make an impact is to put our focus on the circumstances and the environment of the plant. Water the soil often enough, but not too often. Put in some nutrients from time to time. Give the plant a lot of sunlight and during the winter season, use artificial light. And in case I grow peppers indoors, the plants will need a fan to ventilate the leaves. That way the stem grows thicker and has a chance of bearing more pods later.

Yes, I know, I've already talked about this at the beginning. But I am more than willing to repeat myself with the most important parts here! The same principle of crafting the circumstances and the environment applies to organisations and their culture too. Our social construct and ideas living in it are indeed a thing to cultivate to ever higher levels.

The common thing with developing culture is painful, though. It's going to take time, patience and repetition. In fact you build culture just like you would build a muscle. Rep after rep after rep.

The Unlikely Snowball Effect.

I love it when it snows. The last time it did, I made a snowman with the kids. Rolling huge snowballs out of the wet and screeching snow is easy. As a result, our snowmen become quite massive. We typically start with a snowball that we can hold in the palm of our hand. We then roll the ball in the snow to make it bigger. The process somehow reminds me of spinning cotton candy.

In the beginning, the ball multiplies with just a little effort. As the ball gets bigger and bigger, things start to slow down. Eventually, it starts to take more effort to keep the ball rolling, and it becomes harder to notice if it grows at all. The kids lose their interest first. The effort required to produce visible result starts to outweigh the results themselves. However, it is clear that those who believe in the process instead of their thoughts, build the best snowmen.

The same holds true for studying, hobbies, software projects, blogging and pretty much everything where we aim for level ups. If you ever face a crisis of faith, remember that the thing defining our success is a decision. What will you do when the change becomes difficult to notice? Do you trust or discard the process of developing culture and growth? Do you still have faith in the repetition? Rep after rep after rep.

The Road to the Peak of your Profession

I'm a software testing professional and I've taken the same Rapid Software Testing course, three times now. The first time I took the three-day course given by Michael Bolton, it not only changed my view of the world as a tester but also as a human being.

The same thing happened on James Bach's course a little later. Suddenly, I saw the world in colour. Testing had transformed itself from an engineer's toil to an actual hustle of gurus. And now I'm planning on taking the course yet again.

It's the same with every field of expertise. For example, Brian Tracy's training courses to salespeople are just as amazing. The stories are so compelling that even the most resistant monkeys are drawn to the light. The value of work, be it the tester or the salesperson, emerges from how successfully we serve the people around us. After each seminar, talk or training I attend, however, I cannot help but hear the muttering from somewhere in the back of the room.

"Bah. Nothing new! I knew all of it already!"

Most often these words come from the last row. I've also noticed that most of the people muttering have no notebooks with them, or if they do, their pages are empty as some kind of proof of a self-excellence illusion. Often, the quality of their work does not speak for itself either.

The peak of any profession shares one characteristic in common. To every outstanding professional, the basics are incredibly important. That is why a guru gravitates towards things familiar. Time after time they search and research the things they already think they know. Time after time. Rep after rep.

You Can Never Swim in the Same Ocean Twice.

A curious saying, I admit. I've always considered it to mean that the conditions in the ocean will never be the same the next time I hit the waves. I love ice swimming. The water is at freezing point and it always thrills me to dip in. But that hasn't always been the case. The first time I did it, it felt terrible. I screamed and ran as fast as I could back to the sauna. Afterwards the feeling is amazing though, that's why I went for a second run, and then for a third one. Repeating the exercise was a way to condition myself into associating the pleasure with the freezing experience and it worked.

So the water and the conditions are not the only thing to change. My relationship with the water and the conditions are now different too. Repetition is truly the mother of all learning.

The relationship to repetition is crystallised by a simple, yet powerful thought in an Under Armour ad you can find on Youtube. The sports brand invited the legendary Olympic swimmer, Michael Phelps for some collaboration. The video gave us a sneak peak into the everyday life of a champion. I really suggest you check it out.

The closing scene had me sitting silently in front of the screen for a long time.

> "It's what you do in the dark, that puts you into the light."
>
> -Michael Phelps

The Mechanics of a Breakthrough.

"Easy for him! He got lucky" they said.

I've heard friends and strangers say it too many times over the years. It's just that luck tends to follow people like Michael Phelps. People who work hard and day by day tweak the odds in their favour. Until one day, Lady Fortune seems to gaze favourably upon them. Breakthroughs never follow our instructions. It doesn't come fast or cheap, and it has the stigma of first offering failures in formidable amounts even though wannabe-social-media-life-coaches would have you think otherwise. Most of the advice I see in testing, and basically every other walk of life too, looks like this.

Most people can draw those two circles, but those aren't the key to success. Drawing an owl requires thousands of tiny decisions, which all answer one question. What does the owl truly look like?

It is not possible to draw the owl if you cannot see it through your mind's eye. The same rings true for testing. The world is full of tips and teachings on how we should do it. Before you can begin, however, you first need to see in your mind how professional testing looks and feels. But, how then, does one learn to see it? How do we learn to draw the damn owl?

Like with all things in life. You start with a circle, and then you draw, erase, redraw, erase a little, then draw some more. Even if the

wannabe-coaches claim shortcuts to your dreams, I've got to say this! There are no shortcuts to truly embody what you know. There are no shortcuts to skill.

Picasso in his time, for example created a total of 12,000 drawings, 1,800 paintings, 2,800 ceramic works and 1,200 sculptures. If you're not completely dumb, there is absolutely no way to not get good at what you do with this kind of scoreboard. Most of Picasso's work is really bad. Some would even call them failures. But I must repeat myself now. There are no shortcuts to mastery. So basically, to succeed, we must make failure our bitch. The only way to fail for sure is to give up. Or refuse to try in the first place.

Humans have a hard-coded tendency to avoid pain even though we know patience is the key almost every time. The reason why I talk about pain and patience in the same sentence is this. Patience originates from the same word as patient and passion. The Latin origin points to suffering. Passio. Patience means that we are ready to suffer to reach our goals. It means that we pay the price for the breakthrough in full and up front, even though the breakthrough remains uncertain. It's all about trusting the process when changes become harder to notice. Of course, we still need that small pinch of luck to push us through.

Breakthroughs also have the tendency to take us by surprise. Around 10–18 months after the epic failure to be more precise as business and personal development guru Tony Robbins puts it. But to get there, we must learn the one winning method, which can take us across the finish line. Actions are the only way to get results. That is why getting started is the first and the most important skill we can possess. Breakthrough is an inevitable consequence of patiently starting every day until....

If you are tired of starting over with big things in life, this is important. STOP GIVING UP in the first place!

I'm trying to write about software testing here, but for some reason I find myself ranting about success. Still, you might ask what does this have to do with testing? Well, allow me elaborate. If you want a breakthrough, you first need to fall in love with the dance of starting. Embracing the outcomes of your trial and error, then you need to add in a load of patience i.e. willingness to suffer for the results you desire most.

Finally, we come to the testing. Testing is work to tweak the odds in your favour. It is a way to shrink the impact of failures. Sometimes we can see the mistakes through the optics of testing early enough so as to avoid them. Once we understand the mechanics of making a breakthrough, time and probability start playing our game. And later, others can call it luck when we're done.

An outstanding professional does not do or seek new things constantly. Instead, they do things anew constantly. That is what every champion has always done. Baptise your basics and practice patience. Years from now, it will seem like you had a huge head start.

> "Patience, persistence and perspiration make an unbeatable combination for success"
>
> -Napoleon Hill

#3: The Power of Focus

Hey! I've got some good news too. There's no need to worry. Time will take care of it. Just wait.

"Ummm, time will take care of what exactly?"

Time will take care of all the things that do not work. The world will move on. Eventually, stupid wasteful processes and tools will collapse due to their own impossibility. We only need to make sure that better options are available when the time comes.

It will happen for sure when we hit the next recession. When the sales go down and budgets are cut. Stupid ways of working and dull expensive tools will pop out of existence. I can't wait for the next downturn in the economy because that is the time we all have been waiting for. It is the time to hit hard and show everybody the better options. It's our best chance to shine a light on the options that have been ignored for too long.

So prepare yourself. You will need to keep the better options close at hand, so that when the moment is yours so you can strike swiftly. And guess what?! Chances are, you won't even have to wait for the next downturn in the economy for this to happen. According to the Stanley Group study of over 50,000 software companies, only 10% of traditional waterfall model projects and 40% of agile ones succeed. That leaves a hell of a lot room for failures don't you think? Yes, the criteria of success in this study is debatable, but at the same time we know for sure that a large portion of projects fail.

A downturn in the economy or on a smaller scale, a downturn in a project creates a similar vacuum for better ideas to occupy and that is the only moment you need. But in order to seize that day you will need preparation and it's all about the power of focus. Leading a change is always about disrupting the tradition.

Disrupting the Status Quo.

Have you ever thought about the disruptors of our time? How did they succeed in challenging the status quo in the first place? Take for example, businesses like Amazon, Uber and Airbnb. A common thing for disruptors like these is that they all started out with an attempt to build options in the face of the dominating mindset of the hospitality or transport markets. Yes, there were other factors at play for sure, like timing and luck but here is the biggest deal.

The precondition of success is to focus on the solution, not the problem. Basically it means that people and ideas that end up leading, rarely start with an attempt to take down the status quo. Instead, disruption tends to be a byproduct of putting the focus on creating new and awesome things. Both problems and solutions will always be close by because they are just different sides of the same coin. We are only left with a decision. Which side will I choose to guide me?

This makes me think about professional software testing. In testing, we tend to search for problems. We turn our attention to places where something might go wrong and then we report it. We model the bugs, problems and failures in a way that we can easily reproduce the defect at the developer's desk. So basically, we condition ourselves to become problem centric in our everyday work life.

> "We see the things we learn to seek."

This is where we are faced with a hidden occupational hazard. Do you still remember when we talked about the Ford Batmobile? After I bought the new car, everybody suddenly seemed to be driving one, even though I had never seen them before. My perception was biased by the decision I had just made.

In much the same way, for most of our work time in testing, we condition our patterns of perception to see errors in both ideas and implementations. Every day we condition our mind towards seeing problems. As if finding what's wrong wasn't hardcoded in the brain already. The evolution or the lizard brain has us wired for survival first, not for happiness.

> "To me professional testing is playing around with mental health. We might even say we are sacrificing ours so that others may gain."

But now let's look at leading a change. If we want to change the mindset of other people, the problem centric approach just does not work. We should not focus in taking down the status quo nor should we point out the mistakes of other people. It's mostly annoying, no matter how constructive we think we are.

Instead we should learn to think like a true disruptor. In my experience, this is what the best and most respected testing professionals have either accidentally found or deliberately chosen for themselves. We testers are the experts in modelling the world around us. We have an exceptional skill to explain what steps are needed to reproduce something. If we can model the steps needed to reproduce problems, why would we not chip in our know-how with incredible success too? We must learn to direct our own focus and the focus of our peers towards creating better options, towards solutions.

> "Don't worry about failure, because failure will take care of itself. Focus on success!"
>
> -Henry Cavill, Superman

True change for the better is never a matter of common sense or our ability to spot problems. If that was the case, the world would already seem like paradise. Problem spotting is already hard coded into the brain and common sense is trampled by the four human factors we discussed earlier. Remember James M. Buchanan?

Virtually every time, a true change is a matter of our skill in leading the culture. Culture, above all else, is led by the stories we tell, in other words, the Storytools we deploy. So let me ask you this. As a professional, where do you put your focus first? The problems or the solutions? Where should you put it to become who you seek to be?

> "The key to success is to focus our conscious mind on the things we desire not things we fear".
>
> -Brian Tracy

Deploying of the Three

Daring, patience and focus might seem obvious at first. But the thinking mind deems it obvious to cheat ourselves towards easier things to do. Each of the three powers will mean getting far out of our comfort zone, which can be either scary or sweaty. It is either about hard work or getting over an emotional threshold of fear.

Our comfort zone is the place where our activities and behaviour fall into a routine, into a pattern that minimises stress and risk. It provides a state of mental security. There is an obvious benefit to staying comfy: a sense of happiness, low feelings of anxiety, and reduced levels of stress hormones to mention few. This state is beneficial to us, as it gives us the chance to recoup and recover. The problem is, it's not really creative or productive.

All things in life are either growing or withering. Nothing is stationary. Staying comfortable on our sofa will certainly make the body wither. Muscle mass decreases and the aerobic performance declines. And eventually our mental capacity follows the physical. On the other hand getting out for a brisk walk protects the capacity we already have. Turning the pace up a notch feels uncomfortable as we get further out of our comfort zone. But that's how we truly start to develop our capacity to grow.

The same principle applies to every capacity we need to develop, including daring, patience and focus. The only way to grow is to push it to the limit, recover, push it to the limit and recover once more. This means that to increase our performance we need to increase our stress levels. Not too much, but just enough to make a difference. As with many things, there is an optimal level that will bring us the greatest rewards.

> "We choose to go to the moon not because it's easy, but because it's hard!"
>
> -John F. Kennedy

Quit Playing it Safe

I grew up in a small city that had two huge factories producing pulp for the paper industry. The entire economy of my hometown was based around a century-old industrial complex where trucks transported timber in, and all kinds of paper products were shipped out at the harbour.

How many crates of pulp did you process this week? How many could you have squeezed in if you really tried? I grew up to become a software professional just to face those same questions. How many test cases did you run this week?

At the beginning of my software career the whole testing process seemed like it was an industrial assembly line. The organisation chart was almost the same as the factories back home. And, so were the methods of measurement and management. Throughput and efficiency were the numbers where we focused the most. Hence came the questions. How many crates/cases could you have squeezed in, if you really tried?

I would say that one of the biggest professional epiphanies for me was to realise that testing at its core is not about assuring others of the excellence of our product. It's not about producing evidence about the efficiency of our assembly line. And it most certainly is not to serve the industrial complex with its age-old structures.

Instead, testing must shine a light on the things that have remained unseen. Testing tells the truth and pulls people out of the matrix. It is a way of life. It is a journey of exploration and creation.

Now, I can rightly say that testing is changing. It is only natural that the transformation is not going to be easy. The lizard brain is convincing. It tells us to play it safe, keep our heads down, inside your stupid cubicle, to stay on familiar terrain where unexpected things won't happen. Too many times I've met with testers who tell me that test automation just doesn't feel like their thing. Or that exploratory testing feels like the aimless roaming of a cowboy. Or that they aren't comfortable with the code and don't quite understand it.

I say those are the bullshit stories that we first tell ourselves and then live up to them. It is a prime example of the brain playing it safe. Those stories are a stance of survival that will slow down the process of growth, learning and creativity. That is something a next level tester does not tolerate. To me it seems evident that we won't be working in the industry of testing anymore. We testing professionals must transform into the craftsmen of our art, or we will slowly and surely become obsolete parts of an age-old assembly line. And guess what? Art is something that you don't manage. Try to manage a factory worker, and he might stay. Try managing an artist, and he will leave. Testing is not about managing an industrial process. Testing is about leading a creative one.

By doing the things we've always done, we'll get the same results that we've always got. Is that really enough here? Would now be a great time to discard the lizard brain and start telling a new story of the professional you?

Farewell

Guess what? It's September and I just picked the last ripe chili pods of the season. Now it's time to prepare the soil for some new seeds. It's also time for us to go our separate ways. My eyes turn to you in expectation. It's your turn to choose the seeds that you know must be shared and planted.

Care for them and see how they grow to provide better crops than you could have ever imagined. I wish you all the best.

Yours truly.

- Antti